Lessons on
Leadership

Lessons on Leadership

THE **7 FUNDAMENTAL MANAGEMENT SKILLS** FOR **LEADERS AT ALL LEVELS**

by Jack Stahl

KAPLAN

PUBLISHING

New York

Editorial Director: Jennifer Farthing
Acquisition Editor: Shannon Berning
Development Editor: Joshua Martino
Production Editor: Julio Espin
Production Designer: Todd Bowman
Cover Designer: Rod Hernandez

Published by Kaplan Publishing, a division of Kaplan, Inc.
1 Liberty Plaza, 24th Floor
New York, NY 10006

Printed in the United States of America

July 2007
07 08 09 10 9 8 7 6 5 4 3 2 1

ISBN 13: 978-0-7931-9474-2

Dedication

To Sam and Katie with love,
and to the many others who have helped me learn.

Contents

FRAMEWORK 3

Developing People   61

FRAMEWORK 4

Brand Positioning with Consumers   83

FRAMEWORK 5

Customer Relationship Management   107

FRAMEWORK 6

Financial Strategy and Management   133

FRAMEWORK 7

Influencing People   159

Acknowledgments

I would like to thank author/journalist Carol Jose, my editor and writing coach, for her knowledge, skills, great work, conviction, and perseverance in helping me transform my learning, experiences, and initial writings into *Lessons on Leadership*.

Thank you very much Doris Michaels, my agent at DSM Agency. Doris artfully and effectively pushed me hard to bring more of my stories and ultimately more of myself into the book, all the while leading me calmly and sensibly through the process of completing the project.

Another thank you goes to Joshua Martino, my development editor at Kaplan Publishing, for his help in strengthening the book.

Finally, thanks to Susan Whitney Smith for her excellent work in helping get my thoughts and words into an initial draft of *Lessons on Leadership*.

Foreword

John Antioco, chairman and CEO, Blockbuster Inc.

Leading a business in today's world can be a little daunting at times, even for those of us who have been doing it for a while. Striking the right balance between maximizing revenues and profitability while managing costs sounds deceptively simple, but getting it right can be infinitely difficult.

At Blockbuster Inc., at our more than 8,000 stores, located in 23 countries, and through our online movie rental service, with some 70,000 employees serving millions of customers each year, we work to find the right balance every day. Nevertheless, on those occasions when the complexity of it all overwhelms me, I take a deep breath and let the business lessons I learned when I was a boy working with my father, a Brooklyn milkman, subconsciously kick in.

My father worked hard. He made it clear that no one ever got successful without trying, and he paid attention to details, such as never selling his customers milk in scratched-up bottles. He also knew intuitively about the importance of differentiating his business from the competition. Anyone could deliver a couple of quarts of milk, so my father offered extra products like orange juice, sour cream, eggs, and cottage cheese. Adding those products made his deliveries more complicated, but it set him apart and gave him a competitive edge. Probably most importantly, my father was focused on making his customers happy. He knew their names. He knew a little bit about their lives. He knew what they wanted, and he did everything in his power to deliver it.

Although I didn't know it at the time, I couldn't have had a better introduction to the business world than riding in that milk truck with my father. I have carried the lessons I learned from him with me into all my jobs, my various management positions, and ultimately into the companies that I have led. All of which goes to say that I believe business and leadership skills can be learned through observing others, just as I learned from observing my father.

In *Lessons on Leadership,* readers have the opportunity to observe one of the best leaders in the business world, Jack Stahl. Based on Jack's experiences in leadership positions at The Coca-Cola Company—and ultimately as president of the company—and as the CEO of Revlon, Inc., *Lessons on Leadership* offers vital lessons for anyone in a leadership position, from building organizational and people capabilities, to brand positioning, customer relationship management, financial strategy and management, and influencing skills.

Interlaced throughout the lessons of this book are Jack's insights from his real-world experiences at Coke and Revlon. There are also user-friendly techniques that enable readers to be effective, whether newcomers to the world of business and leadership or working to hone their skills.

In today's very competitive environment, business leaders need to take advantage of every opportunity to help them improve their skills. Jack Stahl's *Lessons on Leadership* is just such an opportunity; it can give you the tools to help both you and your organization achieve your goals.

Introduction

Have you ever looked for help in successfully leading and managing your business? This book is the result of years of personal experience in building and leading the right teams for achieving great results. *Results,* not unfulfilled potential, are what the shareowners of an organization want and expect. That requires skilled people and a capable organization focused on setting a bold destination and executing a plan to achieve results. That's what *Lessons on Leadership* is about.

The seven fundamental management skills that I call "frameworks" are designed to help you succeed in a number of challenging organizational and business leadership situations. I believe that my frameworks for leadership can bring you additional focus and enhanced management skills for developing your team and building your organization's capabilities for achieving great and lasting results.

These frameworks have evolved from my own experiences in the corporate world, and as a result of what I learned from some exceptional leaders and mentors early in my career. In sharing these experiences with you, I believe you will be able to advance ahead of the learning curve to leadership success.

The frameworks presented here cover seven basic business areas:

1. Leadership and management

2. Creating a high-capability organization

3. Developing people

4. Brand positioning with consumers

5. Customer relationship management

6. Financial strategy and management

7. Influencing people

I've included in each chapter the specific leadership and management techniques that I believe are most relevant to each framework, and highlighted Leadership Insights, Key Points, and Questions to Consider. These techniques and the highlighted insights, points, and questions are the result of my own experiences as a continuously developing leader. I use them throughout the book as examples to illustrate the techniques that make up each framework. Included at the back of the book for your convenience is an Executive Abstract and Quick Reference Guide for each framework. I thought that an abbreviated version of the frameworks would help you keep in mind the book's larger themes as you go about the daily business of leadership.

For readers already in a management and leadership role, whether you work in businesses, nonprofit, community leadership, or government, these frameworks provide practical insights and solutions to the critical issues that most people, from new employees to business managers and executives, encounter on a daily basis and general advice to influence the way you think. The situations that I describe were, and are still, part of my day-to-day work in managing projects and people to success, just as you are doing.

Many of us in leadership positions that carry heavy responsibility experience emotional highs and lows and periods of self-doubt or indecision, particularly when we face significant changes in addition to the "normal" ongoing pressure to produce outstanding results. During these times, it is important for leaders to react to these pressures in a balanced and thoughtful way. From an emotional standpoint, staying positive and "right down the middle" can be a stabilizing force that not only sets a great example for the organization, but also gives its people confidence and helps them find solutions faster. Being able to play the role of an emotional touchstone for your people is in large part tied to the underlying leadership skills a person brings to difficult periods. It is my goal, through these frameworks, to help you recognize, develop, and sharpen those skills in yourself—as a leader or future leader—and also to help your organization create other leaders.

This book is *not* an attempt to change your personality or style. I believe you will maximize your success by being *yourself* while at the same time utilizing these important skills.

The skills on which I chose to focus were critical to my own growth, and they are the techniques that I believe contribute most significantly to the success of the majority of managers, executives, businesses, and organizations. Obviously, leaders must leverage and integrate the many departments that are critical to organizations—such as production, distribution, and public relations—and although I don't delve into them in detail, many of the guiding leadership principles contained here are relevant to managing any function.

My experience includes 22 years at The Coca-Cola Company, where I worked from 1979 until 2001. During that time, I was fortunate to be afforded a clear vision of what was required to succeed at Coca-Cola, and I was coached by some remarkable leaders. Particularly from mentors like the late Coca-Cola Company CEO Roberto Goizueta and former CEO Doug Ivester I received the lessons, feedback, and advice that developed the core skills that I believe enabled me to be a successful leader. These mentors made me aware of areas that I needed to develop and pointed out my mistakes as they encouraged the growth of my skills. They were masters at managing situationally as well as strategically and their real-world lessons, many of which I share in these frameworks, expanded upon the more technical economics and finance training that I received in the classroom. I can only hope I was a good student.

I was fortunate to work at Coca-Cola during a period of significant growth for the company. Our growth rate in earnings per share increased from an average historical rate of approximately 10 percent per year to more than 15 percent, a dramatic jump. While working at

Coke, the market value of the company increased from about $3 billion to more than $125 billion. Along the way, and ultimately as president of the company, I had a rare opportunity to play a role in Coca-Cola's ongoing success. As gratifying as Coke's success was, it was just as fulfilling to work for a wonderful company with such outstanding people, many of whom shaped my thinking while I helped shape theirs.

My experience also includes almost five years with Revlon, Inc., a company, like Coca-Cola, known for its wonderful brands. My time at Revlon offered me and my outstanding leadership team the opportunity to strengthen the strategies and capabilities of the company so that the company's marketplace and financial results would fully match the long-time strength and appeal of its brands. It also gave me the opportunity to work with Revlon chairman Ronald Perelman, a tremendously successful investor and businessperson. Revlon had experienced a period of slow growth relative to its competitors, and Mr. Perelman helped me learn a great deal about being effective in times that call for fast action and change. Although I ultimately left the company, I am proud to say that while I worked at Revlon, we grew market share, reversing past declines, reduced debt, and positioned the company for significantly improved profitability under its current, very capable leadership team.

Because I gained much of my experience in large corporations with significant resources, my advice may not seem entirely relevant to those of you in smaller organizations or nonprofit agencies, where resources may be scarce. I believe, however, that organizational dynamics are often similar in different environments, and most of the important leadership skills and techniques presented here will apply across diverse organizations large and small, and to various management roles. The frameworks are guidelines that I know have helped me. I believe they crystallize many skills and techniques that leaders practice—some without even knowing it—that enable a leader to maintain the emotional middle ground, avoiding the swings that can limit the success of employees, the leader, and eventually the entire organization. Of course, no book can take the place of solid, hands-on experience. Living with the consequences of mistakes, recovering from them, and enjoying the feeling that comes with success are perhaps life's best lessons. In the following pages, *Lessons on Leadership* will offer you my insights to leadership skill building that will help you enjoy that wonderful feeling of success sooner and more often.

—Jack Stahl

Leadership and Management

I believe that the keys to any successful organization are the **quality of its leadership and its ability to effectively devise and execute a plan.** The long-term health of your organization will be driven by the strength of its leadership—not just at the top, but also in every division or department and at each level of the organization.

This first framework provides important techniques and examples for you and other managers in your organization to deliver strong leadership. Strong leaders can drive your organization's results beyond expectations. The first step is to envision and set a compelling destination for your particular organization. Next, you need a strong, focused strategy and plan. Your plan should include clear interim objectives to execute your strategy, which will keep moving you toward your destination. Communicating your strategy and plan, executing effectively with the help of a strong team, and establishing effective control systems can produce outstanding results for your organization.

In this and subsequent frameworks, I'll share some of the techniques, leadership insights, and key points I've learned and have relied on in my various leadership roles at The Coca-Cola Company and Revlon. I'll also use some anecdotes and examples from those experiences, and others that I've observed. They are real stories that I believe illustrate and amplify the techniques presented. I'll also offer questions to trigger additional thinking in these areas.

Here's a checklist of the techniques I'll be covering in the first framework:

1. Set a compelling destination for your organization.

2. Develop a clear and focused strategy.

3. Set measurable objectives for getting there.

4. Develop a thorough plan to execute your strategy.

5. Communicate your strategy for reaching your destination.

6. Execute details and review your progress.

7. Build and utilize effective control and information reporting systems.

8. Actively develop the organization and the people who can help reach the destination.

SET A COMPELLING DESTINATION FOR YOUR ORGANIZATION

You are a leader. Lead by creating an exciting picture of a successful future for your organization and your people. Microsoft's destination was based around the vision of cofounders Bill Gates and Paul Allen that with the right software, the personal computer would be a valuable and desired tool on every desktop and in every home. What is *your* vision of your organization's destination?

The purpose and importance of creating a destination cannot be overstated. People want a sense of what they are striving for and where they are going in order to commit time and energy to achieving great results for an organization. **People without a clear sense of where they are supposed to go will be unproductive or underproductive, wasting the organization's time and money.**

What is a destination? An organizational destination can be defined in terms of your company's position in the marketplace or how you ultimately want your consumers, customers, employees, shareowners, and other groups important to your success to describe your company. FedEx's destination began as one to *serve the needs of its customers when their package "absolutely, positively has to be there overnight."* Since FedEx created that goal-defining slogan, everything the company has done to capture its global market, from concept to advertising, has reflected some aspect of that "absolutely, positively" destination. To give you a more in-depth look at destination setting, I'll explain how we did it at Coca-Cola® North America in 1994, but some background first will help you understand where the company was when we decided to create a new destination for Coca-Cola in North America.

Created more than a century ago, Coca-Cola is probably the best known brand in the world, built on the basis of a beverage product that 1) offers superb taste and refreshment, 2) is genuine (a major advertising campaign referred to Coke as "The Real Thing"), and 3) is great to consume with family and friends. These have always been three important and wonderful attributes that call to mind my own memories of Coke. As a kid at camp in Maine, a friend and I would sneak to the off-limits vending machine to buy an ice-cold six-and-one-half-ounce bottle of Coke. I thought of those satisfying summer days on my first day at The Coca-Cola Company in 1979, when, full of pride and apprehension, I joined a company that wanted to "buy the world a Coke" and offer a young professional a world of career opportunities.

Originally, the beverage was served only at soda fountains. The Coca-Cola Company expanded in the early 1900s when it offered independent business groups or individuals the franchise rights to bottle and distribute Coca-Cola. The Coca-Cola Company sold Coca-Cola syrup to these bottlers, who would then add carbonated water, package the finished product in bottles, and distribute it to retail stores. The bottlers were granted the right to produce and distribute Coca-Cola in finished product form—first in the United States, and then around the world—as the recognition of the beverage and the brand took off. Seven decades of profitable growth ensued.

By the 1970s, many Coca-Cola bottlers were owned by second and third generations of bottling families. Many of the ownership groups that ran the bottling companies were doing an outstanding job, but others were not big enough to be cost-efficient or were doing a less than effective job. In the 1980s, Coca-Cola began to see the consolidation of the ownership of these many bottling franchises and entered 15 years or so of consolidation by acquisition—one large bottler would buy or merge with another and then be acquired by a still-larger bottler, and so on. The number of bottlers shrank and the remaining companies grew larger. As a result, Coca-Cola had a more effective and efficient worldwide bottling system.

Once that consolidation process was underway, the challenge for the company became how best to capitalize on the more effective bottling and distribution system in order to grow the business in the United States and overseas at a faster rate. That was my challenge when I became president of the North American soft drink business at Coca-Cola in 1994. The Coca-Cola leadership team felt we could now start to capitalize on our stronger bottling system and more aggressively grow the business.

I believed that we needed a clear and compelling way to "paint" that business opportunity so that all the U.S.-based employees of The Coca-Cola Company and the bottlers could actually see a vivid "picture" of where we could take our business in North America. We wanted something that would enable the company and the bottlers to visualize the organization's destination and understand their role in helping to move toward it. With our key marketing people, we came up with the idea of creating a "360-degree Coca-Cola landscape." Its goal was to suggest and reinforce the role of Coca-Cola as part of the everyday lives of American consumers.

Initially, there were three major themes related to the landscape, themes that drew upon Coca-Cola's historic approach to building its business. Here's how that destination played out:

1. **Increased availability**—We decided Coca-Cola would be made even more readily available in many forms—bottles, cans, cups,

and other packages—to consumers across the country. Many more places would sell Coke and our other products. We'd make our product more available in colleges and workplaces like factories and offices—above and beyond the availability of Coca-Cola products in convenience stores and grocery stores—bringing the product to life in the marketplace, making it more pervasively available.

2. **Marketing the landscape**—All of our marketing would be linked to that landscape. Our 360-degree marketing plan was based on the great taste and refreshment, the genuineness, and the enjoyment of Coca-Cola with family and friends. That meant we were to bring those elements to life wherever Coca-Cola was available. All marketing, advertising, signage, billboards, vending machines, packaging, and point of sale materials in stores, all the way through to uniforms and the signs on Coca-Cola delivery trucks—would reinforce these three qualities of Coca-Cola. Our marketing programs would bring this message to life wherever we appeared in the marketplace.

3. **Being the best business ally to our customers**—This third key element of our 360-degree Coca-Cola landscape destination was to bring to our customers the *best* the industry had to offer in customer service. This meant getting our products to their stores—or restaurants, universities, movie theaters, and other points of availability—on time and properly promoted. We worked very hard to understand the customers' overall business needs, strategies, and objectives, as well as their problems and challenges. That way, when we designed marketing programs for Coca-Cola brands, we could market those brands in a way that helped solve our customers' business challenges and supported *their* strategies for how they marketed their own brand and business. An important building block for being the customers' best business ally was to bring the knowledge of The Coca-Cola Company to them in areas that were valuable to their business. We'd look at any reasonable support our company could offer to

the customer in the way of information or consumer understanding—even offering advice or insight into managing functional areas like finance or human resources. In this way, we built an important network of connections between us and our customers and strengthened important customer relationships, large and small. These relationships were built on trust and a mutual, value-added approach to building our businesses together.

Setting a clear destination at that time for the U.S. Coca-Cola business set the stage for the accelerated growth that followed during the next five years. Work to set a clear destination for your business; it may prove to be an important underpinning for your success.

Leadership Insight

People want to work toward or invest in ideas that are exciting and that they can visualize. Paint a compelling picture of what that success will look and feel like to your people.

One approach to developing an overall organizational destination is to **visualize and define how you want each of your organization's key constituencies to view you** in the future. For example, a destination for your shareowners might be your company's pledge to provide above-average rates of return for an extended period of time. A destination for your customers could be your commitment to become their best supplier. These destinations provide a sight-line for various parts of your organization to shoot for and plan toward. The destinations developed for each key constituency should be linked to the overall destination of your organization.

Be imaginative, bold, and aggressive in setting a destination for your organization. By doing so, you increase the chances of maximizing your success. Setting a bold and aggressive destination also will encourage the best thinking from the people in your organization as they look for ways to develop the most effective and creative strategies to achieve your destination.

The masterminds of Home Depot's destination proved that an idea could succeed even though it had never been tried. Cofounder Bernie Marcus dreamed aloud of wide-open warehouse stores where amateurs and professionals could shop for homebuilding supplies. With cofounder Arthur Blank and others, he created Home Depot, a retail organization that has gone far beyond anyone's expectations.

> ### Key Point
> *A modest view of your future brings modest results and rewards. Think big and give people the opportunity to win big.*

Key Question to Consider

Are you involving others in the development of your destination statement? The "buy-in," or personal involvement, of others from the start is important. High performers want ownership of where they are going. Think about how you want to create involvement and buy-in. The process can be as simple as holding meetings with your leadership team and a diverse cross-section of people from your organization where you lay out your preliminary thoughts about the direction you think the organization should go. Encourage smaller breakout meetings where people can hatch ideas, offer suggestions or objections, and generally improve or expand the initial thinking.

As we worked to build and develop a strong destination at Revlon, we initially drafted a statement that called for our company to be "a global beauty leader, led by color cosmetics, driven by our passion for our exciting brands, creativity, and quality." That initially became our destination statement, but we soon found it didn't have the "punch" to motivate an organization. So we asked all Revlon employees to give our Operating

Committee their input to visualize a more compelling business destination. They were encouraged to leave me an email or voicemail with their suggestions for a more compelling destination. We received several hundred ideas. Obviously, we did not include all of them; I remember a particularly passionate voicemail that suggested we focus significant marketing resources towards men to capitalize on the growing market for men's grooming products. Yet, this move would have likely caused us to take our eye off our core business of meeting women's beauty needs, which required significant focus. Nevertheless, I was happy with the number and overall quality of responses, which said to me that many people felt strongly that they had a stake in our future. We shaped the best of the input into an exciting statement of direction. I learned that by opening the dialogue to a wider, more diverse audience, we could create a better and more compelling business destination—one that was tied to Revlon's passion and excitement for our brands. We ultimately chose to express our business destination as "delivering the promise of beauty" to our consumers, customers, employees, and shareowners.

"Delivering the promise of beauty" meant that our job was to deliver the excitement and the innovation of Revlon brands to *consumers*. Another critical step was "delivering the promise of beauty" to our *customers* by becoming their best business ally, which, as I experienced at Coca-Cola, we would achieve by offering innovative customer solutions. Reaching Revlon's destination for "delivering the promise of beauty" to *employees* meant working to become one of the top 100 places to work as ranked by *Fortune* magazine, an aggressive destination. Finally, the destination of "delivering the promise of beauty" to our *shareowners* meant delivering excellent profitability over a long period of time and creating shareowner value for those who owned our business.

By setting these specific goals for Revlon around the idea of "delivering the promise of beauty," it was easy for everyone in the company to visualize what we were trying to do for each of our important constituencies, which enabled each employee to understand our strategies to move us in that direction. These strategies ultimately led to improved revenue and market share performance for the company and its brands.

Leadership Insight

If leaders aren't bold in setting a destination, no one else will be!

As I mentioned, at Coca-Cola in 1994 we set the compelling business destination of creating a "360 degree Coca-Cola landscape." I felt it was important also to *quantify* our business destination, in order to send a message that it would not be "business as usual" for Coca-Cola in North America.

At that time, Coca-Cola had established a market share of just over 40 percent in the United States. We decided to set a business destination to increase our market share to 50 percent by the turn of the century. People within the company, Coke bottlers, and the business press thought that destination was very aggressive—indeed, they were right.

We pointed out that by moving Coca-Cola's market share toward the 50 percent level, we would create efficiencies for the company and Coca-Cola bottlers by growing our business and taking full advantage of our existing resources and infrastructure. That strategy would result in long-term profit growth and value creation for The Coca-Cola Company and the bottlers. That aggressive destination also led to the company and the bottlers investing more in vending machines, hiring more salespeople, and creating new advertising and marketing programs that would have more impact, and required more aggressive new product development to meet the increased needs of consumers.

When 2000 arrived, Coca-Cola's market share had increased from 40 to nearly 45 percent, halfway to our "ten-point increase in market share" destination. While we may not have made it all the way to the 50 percent goal, I believe the company advanced further than it would have had we *not* set such an aggressive destination. Set aggressive, yet achievable targets for your business; it will help maximize long-term results.

DEVELOP A CLEAR AND FOCUSED STRATEGY

Good strategy provides focused corridors for action. Once your destination is set, developing a strategy to reach it is critical. Strategy development means deciding the best way to move your organization towards its destination. You and your team members must review, understand, and take into account your organization's strengths, weaknesses, and the environment in which it operates. Then, consider and develop a range of approaches to move you towards your destination. Finally, select the approach that will most likely maximize the results you seek with an acceptable level of risk for your organization.

At Coca-Cola in the early 1980s, we had a clear strategy to build our brand. The most important strategic pillar was to set up a large, publicly held bottling company for most of the production, distribution, and sales of company products in North America. This was a significant, strategic shift. In the past, locally owned and situated bottlers typically served the community.

By utilizing public ownership capital to create a large public bottler called Coca-Cola Enterprises, we ensured that owners of the smaller local bottling franchises would more likely have a well-funded and ready buyer for their territories if they decided to sell. The new company, Coca-Cola Enterprises, evolved into a large bottler that had the ability to capitalize on economies of scale and serve the marketplace efficiently. This strategy has worked very well and allowed Coca-Cola brands to continue to grow beyond their already large base in North America. This critical, strategic pillar underpinned the business destination of making Coca-Cola brands pervasive in the marketplace, creating a 360-degree Coca-Cola landscape. A well-defined business destination supported by sound strategy enabled us to execute well and deliver stronger results for the organization.

Key Question to Consider

Are you making the tough choices about which options to pursue? Good strategy involves making important choices about how to—and how not to—reach your destination. Focus your resources on your strategic choices. Ignore ideas or actions that are outside your strategy.

The company's early leaders chose to focus marketing resources on drinking Coca-Cola "ice cold" because they believed that this was the best way to reinforce the idea of refreshment. Advertising always pictured the brand in this manner, a marketing strategy that led to decades of growth.

Key Point

Develop a clear strategy that will galvanize people and require them to focus on the right actions for success.

At Revlon, a key part of our strategy was to position our brands around the idea of creating a feeling of "confident sexiness" for our target consumers. We then set a direction that every marketing touch-point would reinforce the new Revlon brand positioning. We charged everyone in the organization with making sure all our advertising, point of sale materials, packaging, and in-store activity reflected the overall brand positioning of "confident sexiness," and were consistent with the brand's character. To do so, we set up weekly new product review meetings that included our marketing, sales, operations, research and development, and legal departments. We reviewed for upcoming product launches the packaging, advertising, and in-store promotions as well as the product itself, all to ensure that each element of the launch plan was consistent with our brand positioning and overall strategy. However, our review meetings were limited to about 20 people, so we encouraged *all* of our employees to report instances where our products were poorly merchandised (displayed for consumers) as they came across Revlon products while they shopped.

By clearly spelling out our brand positioning and strategy, the Revlon organization could take steps to ensure that all our marketing touch-points reinforced them. There was no way that only the senior leadership of Revlon could have ensured that, given all the brands, marketing tools, and activities undertaken by our large, diverse, and worldwide organization. How you reinforce your organization's strategy will depend upon the nature and size of your business, but like my experience at Revlon and Coca-Cola, you and your leadership team should require routine meetings, reviews, and updates to ensure consistent execution of your strategy.

SET MEASURABLE OBJECTIVES FOR GETTING THERE

Measurable objectives are a *quantifiable* means of determining and measuring progress. They will tell you if you are moving towards your destination at the right pace. These objectives might be set in terms of market share, revenue growth, financial results, profitability, customer satisfaction, or any other meaningful checkpoints that measure your organization's progress—or lack thereof.

Leadership Insight

Quantifying a goal forces clarity in discussions about what is possible and what is required to achieve it.

Key Question to Consider

Are you setting objectives that will appropriately "push" your organization? As a leader, your standards count most when objectives are set. If you believe that your organization is best served by aggressive or "stretch" objectives, then aim high! It may be better to reach only 80 percent of an aggressive objective than to outperform a conservative one. At Coca-Cola North America, we set an objective of growing unit sales volume at 8 percent a year; doing this called for and encouraged new thinking and actions. Even though we "only" achieved an average sales growth rate of 6 percent, that increase was well beyond what we would have achieved by being less aggressive. It was also well above the 3 to 4 percent growth rate we had achieved historically.

DEVELOP A THOROUGH PLAN TO EXECUTE YOUR STRATEGY

Your plan should answer the following questions:

- **Assets**—What do you have to work with to achieve your strategy? Examples of your assets might include a strong brand, a solid distribution system, or excellent customer relationships. Your plan should capitalize on your key assets.
- **Action steps**—Who must take what specific steps and by when?
- **Barriers**—What can stand in your way? Examples of such barriers include structural weaknesses in your organization, strained customer relationships, or a weakened position in the marketplace.
- **Resources and solutions**—How can you overcome the barriers?
- **Expectations and returns**—What do you expect to gain financially or in marketplace results?

Every area and function in your organization should develop detailed and thorough plans tied into the overall business plan. For example, you should provide a strategy for human resources that asks:

- How many additional people might this plan require?
- What skills must they possess?
- How do you get those people and skills in place?

- What are the projected costs and expected financial benefits of the additional people?

Beginning in the early 1980s at Coca-Cola, we routinely developed a forward-thinking, three-year plan every 12 months with a particular focus on the next calendar year. The senior leadership of the company reviewed the plan every fall. We spent about half a day with each of 30 geographic divisions from around the world. The process led to better thinking and planning and ultimately positioned the company for double-digit earnings growth over the next 15 years.

Key Point

Require staff functions to develop clear plans to achieve your organization's overall objectives and strategies.

One of these three-year plans led to Coca-Cola's joint venture with Nestlé in 1991. We realized that our strategy called for development of new products beyond our traditional carbonated soft drinks, but the company did not have all the necessary assets and resources in place to develop them.

The company's plan called for Coca-Cola and Nestlé to develop prepared, ready-to-drink coffee and tea beverages in the fast-growing noncarbonated segment of the beverage marketplace. By setting up a joint venture with Nestlé, Coca-Cola could make available its marketing capability and facilitate access to the Coca-Cola bottling and distribution system. Nestlé made available to the joint venture trademarks like Nescafé, a strong worldwide coffee brand, and Nestea, along with their market expertise. The respective strengths of both companies could be tapped to bring products to the marketplace faster and more profitably.

COMMUNICATE YOUR STRATEGY FOR
REACHING YOUR DESTINATION

Don't expect your people to be "mind readers" in determining your strategy and plans. Create as many opportunities as possible in large and small forums to communicate your organization's direction. When you do, have a clear picture of how you want your audience to react to your communication.

Speakeasy Communications Consulting LLC, a terrific firm based in Atlanta, Georgia, specializing in communications training and coaching, developed one communications model that I have used successfully. It suggests that before a presentation *you must outline explicitly what you want your audience to think, say, or do once they've heard your communication.* Compare what you want your audience to think, say, or do after your presentation to *where they are now.* To do so, work to understand their current concerns and consider any existing assumptions they have already made about your ideas. Only by understanding their present position can you develop a message that will move your audience from A to B, from *where they are now* to *where you want them to go.*

When I am presenting or speaking to an organization, I like to arrive the night before I am to make my presentation. This gives me time to walk around the organization's facilities and talk to people that I encounter to get an idea of what is on their minds. This knowledge allows me to be more aware, responsive, and effective during my presentation because I can compare their concerns to the communication destination I have in mind. The extra time also allows me to make adjustments to my remarks so that they will have maximum impact. On one occasion, before I presented to a sales organization, I encountered skepticism about an aggressive sales growth target for the upcoming year. By uncovering the issue in advance, I was able to tackle it head-on by changing my presentation to include information about how each element of our business plan, including new products, advertising, and promotions, could be reasonably expected to enable the growth we targeted.

Before a large employee conference earlier in my career, I learned that some of the employees at Coca-Cola who had been with the company for years believed that we focused too much on the contributions of our newer employees. When the meeting began, I asked who in the room our longest serving employee was. I asked him to stand and be recognized for his contributions and dedication to the company. My message to all about the importance of *every* employee was well received. Work to understand your audience, thereby maximizing your impact.

> ### Leadership Insight
> *Understanding where people stand on an issue allows you to develop a plan to influence where they end up.*

Framework 7, Influencing People, expands on this important technique of how to frame your approach to communicating to achieve effective influence.

Key Questions to Consider

Are you doing enough listening? Make sure that you listen more than speak. In my leadership positions, I have learned that it is easy to communicate one on one with more than 100 people every week. Whether in informal conversations in elevators, over lunch, or leaving the office at the end of the day, people need to understand that you are open to talking with them. Only then will they be forthright in communicating with you. In one casual conversation at Revlon, an employee reminded me that Revlon's U.S. retailers were preparing to install in their stores a newly designed merchandising fixture to hold our cosmetic products. She suggested that I consider asking all of our New York employees, including our senior leaders, to spend a day installing the new fixture in the stores of a major New York City drug store chain. This turned out to be a wonderful idea! What you learn by asking questions of your staff and your customers can be invaluable.

Are you using visible signals to demonstrate your direction? Get personally and directly involved with visible actions that demonstrate your strategy is alive and underway. There are many ways to send signals about your direction, from actions in the area of human resources, all the way to marketing, as the following examples illustrate.

When I was chief financial officer of Coca-Cola, I needed to hire an executive assistant. This is an important role in the company because the position requires managing significant projects and representing the financial department in a number of key meetings. At the time, my department was determined to increase the diversity of its leadership team. After interviewing a broad number of people, it became clear that the candidate with the best skills was a young, African American professional, I wasted no time in offering him the position, and he accepted. His excellent qualifications and subsequent strong performance in the job sent a strong signal that I was personally committed to our diversity initiative and that there were excellent, well-qualified candidates available from across the cultural spectrum.

In another example, when we changed our strategy at Coca-Cola to broaden our beverage business and include teas, waters, sports drinks, and other new beverages, it was very important to demonstrate early success with some symbolic, "quick hit" new product introductions. We introduced these products on a small scale, so that we could move quickly and be able to point to early victories.

Leadership Insight

Early in a change process, it is critical to take actions that demonstrate your direction clearly. People are looking for visible signals of change and progress.

In 2002, my first year at Revlon, it was important to demonstrate to our retail customers that Revlon was going to lead the way with exciting marketing and increased in-store activity. We used the "quick hit" principle of visual symbolism when we were presented with an opportunity to cross-promote the Revlon brand with the then-upcoming James Bond film *Die Another Day*™ (MGM Studios, Inc.). The film starred actress Halle Berry, one of our beautiful and talented Revlon spokesmodels. The tie-in opportunity was presented to us on relatively short notice. Nevertheless, we believed that the promotion would bring excitement to our retailers. It would also clearly demonstrate that we were serious about aggressively growing Revlon's business and gaining share in the marketplace. We forged ahead with it, despite the inherent risks in executing it properly in such a short time. Revlon built a retailer promotion involving "one-time only products." These were special lipsticks and nail enamels designed specifically for the film promotion and modeled by Halle Berry in our ads. We also created in-store retail sweepstakes promotions connected to the movie and Internet-based tie-ins. The excitement that we generated was terrific, and it grew our business aggressively in the fourth quarter of 2002, an important time to demonstrate to our retailers that Revlon was indeed intent on creating growth and excitement with our brands. Although for several years, Revlon's growth had trailed that of its major competitors, the James Bond tie-in promotion became symbolic of our new energy and our brand message of "confident sexiness" and reignited our brands with important retail customers in the United States.

Of course, the Revlon promotion required extensive resources that many organizations don't have. I give this example simply to encourage you to think outside the box about immediate and impactful ways to energize your particular products or services and improve customer relations. Be sure whatever quick-hit ideas you decide to employ are a visible symbol of your strategy with your employees.

Are you persistent in telling the story? Don't give up! Think of communicating your strategy as trying to cross a river. Like the river, your audience is constantly changing and moving. Only through persistent and continuous communication can your message get across. When the late Ronald Reagan became president of the United States in 1981, his constant hammering of communism reflected his policy toward the Soviet Union. From referring to it as "the evil empire" to demanding, "Mr. Gorbachev, tear down this wall!" Reagan used relentless communication during his entire term to inform and inspire.

Are you managing perceptions, or being victimized by them?

People make decisions based on *their* perceptions, not yours. Let your learning about those perceptions shape your communication. Still, while it is important to hear what people are thinking, it's also important to recognize in the early stages of redirecting your strategy that you need to have conviction. At Revlon, our message was that we could strengthen our brands by focusing on our consumers, our customers, our own workplace, and by capitalizing on the power of our Revlon brands. While outside critics of the company (including much of the financial press) were skeptical because of our recent history of relatively slow growth, the operating leadership stayed focused on our core message. Therefore, while being attentive to everyone—including skeptics—is important, it's equally important that you maintain conviction and be consistent about your strategy regarding the organization's future.

Are you using comparisons that help people understand your strategy and what you expect it to deliver?

As we began to establish a strategy for redirecting and strengthening our business at Revlon (which meant making a number of dramatic changes), it became important to instill a spirit of confidence and positive expectation in our people. We believed that if we focused on executing our strategy around our three basic pillars—our consumers, our customer relationships, and our workplace—we could strengthen our growth and become a viable, profitable company.

Such progress would take time. Another major company in the beauty industry underwent a strategy shift to strengthen itself. The process took several years, but the company demonstrated better results than the investment community had anticipated. That analogy gave our people the confidence that we could indeed put Revlon on a strong growth track in the years ahead.

Are members of your leadership team following your example in embracing and communicating your organization's destination and strategy? My experience is that it takes *three to four times as much* communication as you think will be necessary to disseminate your strategy effectively to all levels (particularly for larger or geographically dispersed organizations). Make sure your various area and division leaders are involved—you'll get there faster and their participation will hone and improve their core communication skills too.

EXECUTE DETAILS AND REVIEW YOUR PROGRESS

A strong plan is only as good as its execution. Set time aside in your daily routine for meetings to review the progress of important initiatives. At the meetings, *focus on the execution of each key element of the plan*—follow up, ask questions, and ensure that each action in your plan stays on course. Doug Ivester offered one of my most significant leadership learning experiences about execution in managing projects. As chief financial officer of The Coca-Cola Company (and later its chairman and CEO), Doug attended a meeting to review my team's progress in completing a public offering document that was several hundred pages long. Completing the document was necessary to turn a large Coca-Cola bottler into a publicly held company.

Leadership Insight

Successful execution of important plans and projects requires a leader's attention to detail. Be attentive and others will follow your lead—and your business will benefit.

Rather than accept our broad responses to his questions about the status of the project, Doug sat down with us one evening and went through it page by page. When we finished reviewing it, we had counted 187 errors in the document! They included mistakes as basic as forgetting to include a telephone number for the newly created company to more complex omissions and oversights. At the end of a *very* painful and long evening for us with Doug, we had assigned team member names, action items, and due dates to correct each identified omission or gap. We then had a very clear plan for what we needed to do in the following days and weeks.

Key Questions to Consider

Are your employees sweating the details? By focusing on the details, you can ensure processes work better at the lowest level and avoid crises. Doing so might frustrate some people who would prefer that you not be so involved. Yet, once they demonstrate that *they* are sweating the details then you can focus your attention elsewhere.

Are you automatically assuming good execution? Do not assume your plan is being well executed until you've seen a person demonstrate that ability. Until then, review for evidence that plans and strategies are being implemented correctly.

In early 2004, Revlon had an opportunity to strengthen our balance sheet dramatically by offering our debt-holders the chance to exchange their debt for new shares of Revlon common stock. This so-called "debt for equity exchange" would have the effect of reducing Revlon's debt by hundreds of millions of dollars. This project was obviously critical to Revlon's financial health because at that time the company had debt on its balance sheet amounting to almost $2 billion, an inordinately large amount for a company its size. Tom McGuire, our chief financial officer, played a lead role in executing that transaction, along with our very capable legal staff led by Bob Kretzman, our chief legal officer. Tom and Bob established a daily meeting routine with members of the team responsible for executing the transaction. The team included people from finance, legal, and other important functions of the company. They focused on timetables and key actions to be taken during the course of the day and week. That convinced me that they were aggressively managing the project and identifying any problems that needed immediate action. This cross-functional process allowed Revlon to execute the exchange in the course of about 90 days, faster and more smoothly than had we not managed the process so aggressively. Watching Tom and Bob's team in action and observing their careful attention to detail gave *me* the time and ability to focus on other parts of our business.

> ### Key Point
> *Focus extra attention on areas of your organization where the details are not being closely reviewed and managed.*

Are you relentless? High energy, positive attitude, and tenacity count. It is amazing how people will respond to someone who is appropriately persistent, positive, and focused on an objective. People must know you will not back away from what's important, including your standards of success.

At Coca-Cola, a critical part of growing the company's business was outstanding in-store execution—getting product to the store in a timely fashion, getting retailer shelves stocked properly with Coca-Cola products, seeing that the products were "faced," or pointed, in the right direction so the consumer could easily identify our brands, and pulling bottles of Coca-Cola and other products forward on the shelves to be within easy reach of the consumer.

A senior leader of a large Coca-Cola bottler was relentless in this task. He traveled constantly to retail stores, focusing on *quality execution by observing attention to detail.* His energy sent a clear message to his operating managers on both sides of the Atlantic that attention to and execution of details was a critical driver of success. He sent that message out clearly every day by example, through his own constant personal attention to execution at the point of sale. This focus helped accelerate growth and increased market share. Focus your own energy on the details of your business to help drive results.

Are you looking for the cracks? Where are the slow leaks that ultimately turn into a flood? Repair them as soon as you see them. Observe carefully and ask questions to determine how your customers are reacting to the level of service your organization is providing them. Anything less than very positive feedback may indicate a problem that could quickly turn into a big one. One factor important to success at Revlon is the production of our large plastic merchandising fixtures that hold and display our products in retail stores. These fixtures hold anywhere from 600 to 800 SKUs (a stock-keeping unit is a unique product and package combination) of various lipsticks, foundations, eye products, and nail enamels. Getting these fixtures produced and distributed to retailers in time for them to be properly stocked and merchandised with our products in stores is critical.

Not long after joining Revlon, I had occasion to meet with the supplier of our retail fixtures. In the course of that meeting I asked, "Do we have routine meetings in place to coordinate the timely production and distribution of these fixtures to our retail customers?"

He replied, "Well, one important regular Tuesday review meeting between our company and Revlon has been discontinued."

I made a note, and followed up, and I discovered that eliminating that meeting could cause delays in delivering the merchandise fixtures to our customers. Our sales, marketing, and merchandising groups focused on the problem immediately. They reinstated the weekly review meeting with the supplier, which averted problems with Revlon's retailers. In this case, asking a simple question of a supplier about something that might have seemed unimportant identified an issue before it became a problem. It's important for leaders at every level to be observant and to detect *cracks in the execution of details* that can lead to much bigger—and costlier—problems.

Are you relying exclusively on company manuals and rulebooks to guide your people? Don't do this! Try providing clear direction to your people through simple guiding principles that they can carry with them wherever they go. Heavy, thick, and complicated employee manuals cannot go everywhere with employees in their day-to-day activities. Therefore it's wise to communicate your most important company rules and principles in a way that makes them easy to remember and follow.

Some years back, an executive from a resort company and I were talking about creating simple company policies for better customer relations. She gave me an illustration of how her approach to using simple principles worked in managing customer relations. They decided their four most important principles were: 1) Enjoyment—Guests' enjoyment of their visit was paramount; 2) Courtesy—Customers were to be treated courteously at all times; 3) Safety and hygiene—Regulations were to be adhered to without exception; 4) Promptness and efficiency—The customers' needs were to be served as promptly and efficiently as possible. Those four principles were easy to remember and employees could "carry them around" in their heads. One day, one of her employees was cleaning an outdoor area around one of the resorts using power equipment. A guest approached the employee and asked where he could buy a Sprite. Choosing safety first, the employee turned off but did not abandon his cleaning equipment. He directed the guest to a nearby bar by the pool. As the guest walked away toward the pool, the employee promptly used his communications walkie-talkie to call ahead to the bartender before resuming his work. When the guest arrived at the bar, his beverage of choice was poured and ready for him to drink. Imagine his surprise and pleasure! He had been treated courteously and efficiently, his needs had been anticipated, and the experience enhanced his enjoyment of his resort stay. This clever employee team acted on the company's principles in a very creative way. (That they also had facilitated the sale of one of my company's beverages pleased *me*.) Easy-to-remember company principles can really work to encourage action that goes beyond expectations and achieves positive results!

Key Point

Develop clear and simple key principles or values to guide the day-to-day behaviors that will create success for your organization.

Do you act fast? Complete tasks or projects as quickly as you can. In some ways, projects are like minefields—the longer you stay in one, the more likely you are to walk into a problem. Be proactive rather than reactive, and get things done.

We learned this lesson many times at Coca-Cola when taking subsidiaries public. If the process moved too slowly then the financial markets might change so dramatically that we could not complete a successful offering at the price we wanted.

At Revlon, acting quickly to capitalize on the tie-in with the MGM Studios James Bond film helped demonstrate to our retail customers and consumers that Revlon was going to be proactive, and our quickness had a positive impact on sales.

BUILD AND UTILIZE EFFECTIVE CONTROL AND INFORMATION REPORTING SYSTEMS

Good leaders and managers use control and information reporting systems as effective management tools for planning, keeping the execution of the plan on course, and protecting the organization's assets. A control system consists of those routine reports, analyses, review meetings, and audits that are designed to ensure sound decision making and to protect the value of your organization's assets.

Coca-Cola built an effective management information system called the monthly rolling estimate. This process required each of our operating units around the world each month to forecast all the key line items on the profit and loss statement for that month, the quarter, and the remainder of the year. That tool forced significant and frequent conversations about revenues, cost control, and overall profitability. The information was put in the hands of Coca-Cola leadership monthly like clockwork, and created significant management dialogue focused on the direction of the business. It became a central management tool for the leadership of The Coca-Cola Company to ensure we were focused on our key financial objectives, and delivering the results we needed. This rolling estimate process is a fine example of a control and management tool that created real value for Coca-Cola's business during the 1980s and 1990s, and it is still in use today.

Key Question to Consider

Do your control and information reporting systems support your key strategies and plans? Match your reporting systems and "key indicators" to the critical objectives that will drive your plan, and to other significant yardsticks of organizational health, like product quality and brand health.

ACTIVELY DEVELOP THE ORGANIZATION AND THE PEOPLE WHO CAN HELP REACH THE DESTINATION

To reach your destination, your organization must develop and maintain strong capabilities in areas important to your success. To create and maintain strong capabilities in all areas of your organization requires that you select, acquire, develop, and reward people who have, or can acquire quickly, core skills that will be continuously developed as they progress. How to do this is the subject of the next two frameworks.

Key Question to Consider

Are you staying in close touch with your people? Outstanding leaders know that they need to stay in close touch with their people.

Feedback and development occur primarily through focused one-on-one discussions. Yet, the payoffs that arise from quality discussions, many times unplanned, are significant. Let your strong performers see that, as their leader, you are willing to recognize them as individuals who are key to your organization's success. Let them know that you are pleased to be making an investment in them.

CLOSING STATEMENT

Outstanding leaders develop a clear picture of where they want to go and strategize how to get there. They create a clear and focused plan for reaching their destination. Then they attract, manage, and develop the people and resources to make it happen in an effective way. These great leaders make connections between different parts of an organization and the business environment and then ensure quality execution of the details in order to create strong results. They expect and encourage others to do the same. Solid performers seldom want to disappoint a strong leader. Ultimately, effective leaders find ways to celebrate with their people the success that strong leadership and execution brings to the organization, and to reward the achievement of good results.

As you strive to become a strong, effective leader, be aware of the key elements of this first framework and the positive results that using them can result in for you, and your organization. Don't hesitate to seek help or coaching in the areas where you feel your own skills need strengthening. You will enjoy seeing your abilities as a leader increase and yield excellent results.

Creating a
High-Capability
Organization

Whether your leadership creates great results ultimately depends on the overall capabilities of your organization to help shape and execute your plan. *Organizational capability* is your organization's total ability to work together and effectively position and market its products and brands, manage its relationships with its customers, execute financial strategies, and perform other functions critical to its success.

Great performance and results do not happen by accident. They are most often the product of improvements in *overall critical capabilities,* which are driven by the leadership of an organization. However, even good leaders sometimes miss this point: Like sustainable increases in performance, new strategies also require organizational capability shifts.

If the new strategy of your business is to reduce the cost of its products, that strategy may require building new capabilities in efficiently purchasing low-cost raw materials. That may call for new or newly trained people with stronger negotiating skills to bargain for those materials, or perhaps a new *information system* to more closely measure costs and expenses. If your strategy calls for developing more new products, you may need not only to hire more staff in your market research department, but you may also need to change the *process* of creating new products. That means preparing each department or function—marketing, research and development, sales, and manufacturing—to be capable of developing more new products, which will change the work of every department involved.

The most critical step to creating organizational capability, the focus of this chapter, is attracting and retaining people who have the skills and commitment to ensure the organization's success. Once you have them on board, the subject of the third chapter is about developing their skills to ensure that they have the continuing ability to help create success for your organization.

My own experience is that the process of building a strong and capable team of people, takes tremendous energy and time. Sometimes it can take many years, depending on the size and scale of the organization.

At Coca-Cola in the early 1980s, new CEO Roberto Goizueta established a different direction for the company. He called for aggressive earnings-per-share growth of 15 to 20 percent annually, a significant increase from the approximately 10 percent growth that Coca-Cola achieved during the 1970s. Goizueta understood better than prior leaders that a major strategic shift designed to dramatically change company performance required an accompanying dramatic upgrade in organizational capabilities. This upgrade applied to every division and department, including the financial function, which I had recently joined. Our chief financial officer determined that to support Goizueta's strategic shift we would need to track business results faster and more accurately. The CFO also determined that his division would require new personnel with excellent project management and negotiation skills to support the buying and selling of Coca-Cola bottling companies, a key part of executing the new strategy.

That determination resulted in the targeted recruitment of accountants from large and notable public accounting firms. They brought high-level accounting skills that were invaluable in our efforts to strengthen the company's management information systems. Those systems in turn provided excellent support to management as they strived to reach Goizueta's aggressive goal. The financial department also added employees with strong financial analysis and project management skills to enable the process of buying and selling of businesses, such as acquiring independent Coca-Cola bottlers in order to then sell them to other bottlers who were better able to improve Coca-Cola's performance in those markets.

These actions had a significant impact on the overall growth of The Coca-Cola Company over the next decade. The newly defined and then restructured financial function of the company played an important role in that success.

As a young leader, I learned invaluable lessons from participating in that dramatic shift in destination and goals. Specifically, I discovered what is necessary to acquire and assemble a capable team.

The following list represents the key building blocks in creating a high-capability organization:

1. Communicate the opportunity for your business and its people.

2. Be visible to the people in your organization.

3. Present a clear picture of the core skills required for success in your organization.

4. Recruit and assign jobs based on the necessary skills to succeed.

5. Invest in and capitalize on diversity.

From this framework's techniques and insights, you can adapt and hone an approach to building capability specific to the needs of your organization and tailor it to your leadership situation.

COMMUNICATE THE OPPORTUNITY FOR YOUR BUSINESS AND ITS PEOPLE

In order to commit to the goals of your organization and to building its capabilities, your employees need to have a sense of its goals and how they can help achieve them. They should also know that your organization can and will provide opportunity for them to grow their skills and achieve personal success. This understanding not only builds commitment to your organization, but also encourages employees to focus on their own career development. People often look for excuses not to get a job done, particularly when times get tough. Failure to underscore your commitment to your strategy and your people and encourage feedback provides fertile ground for excuses.

When I joined Revlon in early 2002, it was apparent to me that the company owned a wonderful, world-recognized brand that represented glamour, excitement, color, and innovation. Yet, as a company, Revlon had not fully capitalized on the strength of that brand in the previous five or six years. I believe that was due, in large part, to a lack of effective communication across various divisions of the organization. This became apparent to me during my first days at Revlon—as I walked the halls and introduced myself to people, I heard many different views of the company's current direction. Revlon's employees did not have a clear vision of where the company was headed and their role in getting there. Therefore, the company was not capitalizing on the promise of its great brand through excellent marketing and operational execution with its retail customers, and therefore was not maximizing its financial results.

I believed at the outset that if the company could refocus on three key strategic building blocks, Revlon could again become a global beauty leader and move toward profitable growth. These building blocks were to:

A) Capitalize on the strength of our brands with consumers.

B) Be our customers' best ally by delivering real value to our retail partners through innovative customer solutions to help them grow their businesses.

C) Strengthen organization capability and make Revlon one of the top 100 great places to work.

These concepts became the steps to "Delivering the Promise of Beauty." Achieving this destination required that every one of the 6,000 Revlon employees around the world actively participate in executing the strategy. I wanted them to feel personally involved in bringing those three building blocks to life.

Initially, strengthening organization capability was the most important of the three steps. This step involved defining the core skills essential for Revlon's people to have in order to drive success for themselves and the business—I will expand on those particular core skills later in this framework. We also developed performance feedback and compensation systems that *linked to a person's acquisition of those core skills* and created related training. These actions were designed to maximize Revlon's success as a company and ensure that those who helped create that success would share in it through career growth and rewards.

In many organizations, leaders succeed in redefining plans and strategic direction, but time and time again, they fail to develop a clear communication strategy that engages the organization's people in the new direction. Planning and executing this type of communication requires much more work than most leaders anticipate. Unfortunately, poor communications often dooms terrific ideas.

At Revlon, we developed a comprehensive communications program, which I will outline here to give you a sense of what is required to execute such an effort. First, we initiated discussions up, down, and across the organization about our destination and our three strategic building blocks. Our goal was to communicate, get input, achieve buy-in, and create action to execute our new direction in every part of the company.

To accomplish that, initially, members of our operating committee and I held large group meetings in New York and other U.S. locations, including Oxford, North Carolina—our major manufacturing location—and at our main overseas offices. In those meetings, we laid out our destination and strategies and encouraged our employees to offer their reactions. Often in front of their managers, employees brought forth great ideas about the packaging and merchandising of our products. At one of those company wide meetings, an observant employee pointed out that our company introduced far too many products and package alternatives for one of our smaller brands. She pointed out the extra production costs and the additional inventory investment needed to merchandise and market all those SKUs, many of which were "slow movers." Her thoughts highlighted for me the opportunity to streamline our business and create efficiencies within our brands without a significant negative effect on revenues.

While meetings like these may not seem like a particularly novel way of disseminating information to employees, if they follow a period when there has been little communication from an organization's leaders, they can be very powerful in generating the energy to begin building new capabilities. At Revlon, employees routinely expressed their surprise and appreciation for our basic commitment to communicate with them. Because it had been a while since employees had attended these kinds of meetings, it took some real effort to encourage them to break the ice during the comment and question-and-answer period. Often, I would promise lunch with a particularly popular executive or (jokingly) offer an all-expense paid vacation to the employee who spoke up first. In any change process, it is important to recognize that there will always be concerns that will not be brought into the room. To deal with this, I would often ask the group during the discussion period of our meetings to tell me what is *not* being said. In other words, what will be said in the hallway right after the session? By encouraging discussion of that concern during, and not after, the meeting we could deal with it up front, influence it, and not allow the issue to become a barrier. Although some employees will remain on the fence, as a leader your responsibility is to create the energy to push through resistance in the early stages of a change process.

Leadership Insight

People and organizations develop faster with encouragement, when they have a sense of direction, and when they are heard.

As the second step in disseminating our message, I began to write a series of weekly updates describing the company's progress to our employees. The letters were sent to all Revlon employees during the first 12 months of our journey, and they brought a positive response. Revlon's people were surprised that other members of our leadership team and I would regularly take the time to write to them. In each letter, I included very specific examples of the company's progress in the past week. For example, I noted positive news on market share, good feedback from consumers about a new product, or progress on a cost-reduction action. On the other hand, if we missed a key financial target, I discussed that shortfall and why it occurred. I also delineated what had been my own priorities and the focus of the operating committee for the previous week, and where we would be focusing our attention going forward. This served to take some of the mystery out of the senior leadership of the company. Every letter to employees encouraged them to give us ideas to make progress toward our destination.

Adhering to that "tell and retell" adage, after Revlon leadership informed every employee of our destination and they learned about our three strategic building blocks, we layered in a third approach: We began to have a weekly "progress update" meeting. Every Thursday, anyone at Revlon's New York office could meet with members of our leadership team and me to discuss significant company events during the past week. We'd focus on what we had done (or what we'd discovered needed to be done) to strengthen our brands; what had been accomplished to strengthen our execution and innovation with our retail customers; and what was underway to strengthen our organization.

We also learned at those meetings where we fell short in the eyes of our employees. On one occasion, in front of a large group, an employee pointed out that we seemed to be losing energy for some of our people development programs. Attendance had dwindled and the frequency of training programs had diminished, and she questioned the company's commitment. This was a disappointing surprise for me—sometimes leaders lose sight of the workplace programs that are important to employees—but it also was a call to action. Her input compelled me to see that these programs were reemphasized and reenergized. Every week, 40 or 50 people attended those New York meetings. Once a month, we teleconferenced with our facilities around the United States and Canada—like our manufacturing facilities in North Carolina or our distribution facility in Arizona—and employees gathered in conference rooms to participate. They were encouraged to offer questions and perspectives like the New York employees. These meetings reaffirmed our messages throughout the company.

Key Point

Do whatever it takes to help every single person understand your organization's direction and destination.

As we evolved the strategy further, we held quarterly reviews and invited all employees to attend more formal presentations. Revlon employees from many different levels of the company—instead of only the operating committee leadership team—were by and large the ones to give these presentations. This was actually somewhat of a relief to me and other senior leaders; it transferred responsibility for preparing presentations to the people from whom our employees really wanted to hear success stories: each other. Our people enjoyed hearing from the marketing department about consumers' enthusiasm for the new makeup line they helped to produce and sell. They valued listening to operations managers describe the incredibly fast installation of a new automated picking machine in North Carolina. Employee presentations were a strong and popular way to demonstrate that everyone counts and everyone leads at Revlon. The stories inspired other employees and gave them confidence that they, too, could have a positive impact on the direction of our company. This was a key objective of our overall communication strategy.

The success of these communication techniques at Revlon underscored the importance of an aggressive communication plan during the early stages of a change process or turnaround strategy.

At Coca-Cola North America in 1994, strengthening our capabilities was also critical to accelerating our growth. It called for aligning our people around our strategy and direction. To help employees visualize our new destination, we created a large mural to illustrate our destination of a "360-degree Coca-Cola landscape." The colorful mural showed people drinking Coca-Cola throughout their daily lives. We thought it was exciting to portray our product as an integral part of people's lives, enjoying Coca-Cola while working, playing, and at school.

We had prints of the mural made for everyone in the Coca-Cola organization. To my surprise, many employees framed the print and hung it in their offices. I thought people would be reluctant to display them for fear of appearing as if they were "drinking up the party line." I learned instead how much our employees really wanted to know about and identify with their organization and where it could go. The mural served as a reminder as people helped bring that landscape to life where Coca-Cola was sold, including grocery and convenience stores, manufacturing plants, administrative offices, and college campuses.

That grassroots enthusiasm was contagious; I saw it firsthand. Before a visit to a store run by one of our major convenience store customers, I met first with a Coca-Cola bottling company representative who called on that customer. The bottling rep showed me a checklist he had designed for creating a "mini Coca-Cola landscape" right inside that convenience store. He explained that when he got there, he always used his list to check the signage and how the product was arrayed and, if the promotional materials *drove the message* that we were trying to convey in our 360-degree landscape mural—genuineness, great taste and refreshment, and great times with family and friends. He was communicating that destination directly to our retail customer and through them to their customers, the ultimate Coca-Cola consumers.

Our destination was so compelling and well communicated that certainly even our competitors knew where we were going. They saw that we were relentless about our objectives and that it was almost inevitable that we would grow our market share—and we did.

There are many different ways to communicate a destination, strategy, and objectives across an organization. At Coca-Cola, we successfully communicated our business strategy around the idea of a "360-degree landscape." At Revlon, we built a series of communication events and routines. At both companies, we communicated strong and positive energy to employees about our destination and as a result we accelerated the development of organizational capabilities, leading to stronger results.

If you're observant, you'll find formal and informal ways that work for you and your leaders to communicate effectively the direction and progress of your organization.

Key Point

Create easy channels for feedback to ensure that your people understand where the organization is going and that they can influence its direction. Don't allow lack of communication by you and your leadership team to be an excuse for lack of performance or results!

Key Question to Consider

Are you involving all of your people in the process of defining the strategy to reach the destination of your organization? By involving everyone, you may gain new insight and data from them that could shape how you ultimately define and execute your strategy. If you give them a visual picture of the destination and a part in the conception of strategy, they will be more committed, more effective, and more creative in helping you reach your destination.

BE VISIBLE TO THE PEOPLE IN YOUR ORGANIZATION

It always amazes me, the positive buzz that leaders create by simply walking around in their organizations and making themselves visible to their employees each day.

Shortly after I joined Revlon, one of our key strategies was to install new, updated merchandising fixtures in approximately 20,000 retail stores in the United States. We decided that it was important that all of our senior leaders, as well as our employees in the New York City area, had an opportunity to participate in installing these new fixtures at retail outlets because, for one thing, employees at our corporate headquarters could learn more about our products and how they are merchandised as they physically participated in setting up new fixtures in drugstores and other retail outlets. It also provided a way for us to get a jump on the installation process with an important drugstore customer in that area.

I helped install one of these merchandisers at the drugstore adjacent to the Revlon headquarters building in New York City. (Thankfully, I had more experienced people on hand!) It was a terrific experience for me. I enjoyed learning more about Revlon's products and how they are marketed, and it was exciting to play a hands-on role in our new merchandising strategy. I didn't anticipate the positive impact that our leadership team's participation had on our organization. Many people told me that they were glad to see senior management "rolling up its sleeves" to better understand the complexities of executing our merchandising approaches in retailers' stores. We made a positive impact on our organization simply because our company leaders were visible. We were actively involved in the execution of one of our core strategies for our Revlon brand: *being the customer's best ally.*

The event also attracted media attention, which created a public reminder to our retail customers that our leadership team was actively involved with Revlon's day-to-day activities. In addition, it showed that we were intent on changing the culture of our company to link the day-to-day business details of all levels of the company to our retail customers and to consumers of our brands.

These moves created positive energy internally and with our customers. That energy paid off during the early stages of turning our company around after a period of decline and getting it back on the road to progress.

Not long after, I had the opportunity to visit our production facility in North Carolina. I loved being in a production environment and walking the lines to talk with the people who make it happen, day in and day out—creating the products of Revlon, Almay, and other company brands. It was exciting to see the tangible results of product development work in New York. Someone suggested that I work on the production line awhile, and I was glad to try my hand at what other Revlon employees do every day. People were excited that someone from senior leadership from New York, after many years, came to spend time on the production lines. The benefits to my knowledge of our manufacturing process were greater than I could have anticipated. My visit also showed our employees that our management cared about what it takes for them to create success for the Revlon organization on a daily basis. Soon after, our very capable plant manager and his team built on that energy and took it a giant step further. They asked people on the production floor how to reduce unnecessary waste in the production process, and they got dozens of ideas that ultimately saved Revlon millions of dollars annually.

Leadership Insight

In leadership, visibility counts! It demonstrates that you take seriously the importance of working together to reach your organization's destination.

No matter what your level in your organization is, you can—and should—be a personal and caring leader. Show your fellow employees that you care about them as individuals and you care about what it takes for them to do their jobs in order to help achieve the results that you all want for the organization. Respond to the concerns and challenges your people are facing. If they believe that you care enough to be visible and they believe you are personally dedicated to the goals you have set and are trying to achieve together, they will be more willing and effective contributors to your organization's progress.

Even conversations in an elevator can be very important. On one occasion at Coca-Cola after a particularly stressful budget review, a relatively junior employee approached me while we were in the elevator during a break. He said that I had been far too critical of one of the presenters during his financial presentation in front of a large group. When I came back from the break, I publicly apologized to the presenter, which took some of the tension out of an already tense environment. Other times, I learned something in an elevator conversation that changed my approach to a business initiative. This kind of dialogue creates the opportunity for "inexpensive" learning. Capitalize on these opportunities.

Early in my career at Coca-Cola, I often received letters from senior leadership after an important event. Once, following a large meeting with investors, our chairman sent me a note congratulating me on my presentation. He thought my speech gave investors a new way to understand Coca-Cola's opportunity to grow per-capita consumption of our brands internationally, a key to believing in the investment potential of Coca-Cola stock. Of course, I was aware that the chairman of our company was very busy, so I was amazed and impressed that he would take the time to write such a thoughtful letter. Knowing he cared enough to write to me not only reinforced the effort I put into my work, it also strengthened my loyalty to The Coca-Cola Company. Be visible to your organization; it counts!

PRESENT A CLEAR PICTURE OF THE CORE SKILLS REQUIRED FOR SUCCESS IN YOUR ORGANIZATION

Your people will want to know the specific skills they need to be successful in your organization. In the following example, like other examples, I changed the employee's name for reasons of privacy, but her story emphasizes the need to communicate the importance of basic business skills.

Susan was in the marketing department. She was a very good technical marketer—she was creative and she understood how to build brands. What Susan didn't have was a clear picture of the core skills required for success in our company (and, I believe, in most business environments). Clearly, her managers and I had not given her the feedback and coaching that would have helped Susan understand and develop those skills. Perhaps she was most lacking in communication and influencing skills, which are critical for success in marketing. Susan often presented the upcoming year's marketing program to Coca-Cola bottlers. Her presentation included part of our new product plan, advertising, and in-store promotions. Unfortunately, Susan's presentations lacked focus and clarity, and she spoke without energy, which her audience could mistake for a lack of conviction in the marketing plan. As a result, some Coca-Cola bottlers in attendance would not commit their resources to executing the programs with our retail customers.

Susan was considering resigning, but I really didn't want the company to lose her talents. I asked her to come to my office to discuss her situation. I intended to do what I could to keep Susan with us.

At first, we had a relaxed and general conversation. Then, I moved to the issue at hand—I asked, "Why are you thinking about leaving, Susan?"

She was candid: "Because I didn't get the promotion I wanted, Jack, and I think I deserved it. I figured that if the company didn't value me any more than that, it was time for me to move on."

Susan and I discussed her disappointment over missing that promotion, and then we talked about the "why."

I knew that Susan's boss had told her that her communication skills weren't good enough to effectively sell her ideas. That limited her success in her current position, and that was why she hadn't been promoted to the position she wanted.

Susan also admitted to me, "I've been told that sometimes it appears to others that I don't have enough conviction about my marketing ideas."

"Do you think you have conviction about your ideas?"

"I think so—at least I do most of the time—but sometimes I might not communicate my ideas as strongly and effectively as I should."

I could tell from what she had said that her lack of conviction was likely due to low self-confidence in her communication skills. This prevented her from aggressively promoting and defending her ideas, an area that was critical to her work.

"There are communications models that can help you with that skill," I said. "Have you been shown any of them?"

She hadn't. We talked about the Speakeasy communications model that I had used and believed was very effective. I told her I felt that if we had given her feedback and offered this model sooner, she may have been able to sell her ideas when she needed to sell them and earn that promotion. "Well, that may be true," she said. "But it's too late now. Everyone's perception of me here is set. I think I'll be more effective elsewhere. Hopefully I can accomplish my career goals at my new company."

I said, "If you can embrace the communications model and develop that skill, and in fact over time succeed at selling your ideas, I believe that you will have a good chance to realize your career goals right here. Do you think you'll have that same chance at the company you're going to?"

Susan thought, and then she said, "Well, probably not, Jack."

"If you'll change your mind and stay with the company, I will commit to helping you acquire the kind of communication skills you need to move toward those goals," I told her.

Leadership Insight

People focus on those skills and behaviors that leaders say count.

Susan decided to stay. I knew that she hadn't learned the core skills required to succeed with us because we had not helped her learn them, but I knew it would be worth it to the company if we could. If Susan left, the company would have lost someone who had considerable talent.

After she decided to stay, I was able to coach Susan as she worked to develop those core skills. She attended a seminar on developing a focused message for group presentations. She also attended a three-day session on presentation skills that focused on communicating in front of large groups with energy and authority. With the benefit of that training, Susan and I had a common model for communicating effectively and discussing her effectiveness. From then on, after I watched Susan's presentations, I would ask for her own assessment about her communication and give her my own feedback. As a result of coaching, she went on to make significant contributions at Coca-Cola.

I believe there are six core skills necessary for success in most organizations. Other skills that are specific to a profession or are highly technical can be added to the list, but these six apply more universally, which is why I call them the "core" skills. They are the ability to

1. learn from, observe, and question the environment around you;

2. see opportunities;

3. develop a detailed plan and organize the necessary resources for action;

4. execute a plan and focus on the details;

5. effectively communicate and work as part of a team; and

6. recognize and develop the skills of others.

Here's what I believe each of those core skills mean and require. I will use some of my experiences to illustrate how these skills can positively impact you and your organization's performance, capabilities, and bottom line.

Learn from, Observe, and Question the Environment Around You

For people to be creative and responsive to the needs of their business, they need observations and data that can be turned into insight and action. The first step is an attitude of openness and curiosity and a willingness to learn. Reading books, magazines, and newspapers, observing or experiencing other industries, watching television, participating in sports, and enjoying the arts, entertainment, and travel are all opportunities for learning and observation. Family and friends also are sources of ideas and inspiration and might even inspire an idea that you bring to your organization.

For example, packaging ideas coming out of the beauty-care products industry might be carried over into the packaged foods industry. Ideas from the world of clothing and fashion often carry over into the world of cosmetic and beauty products. My early days at Revlon in 2002 coincided with the unfortunate need for heightened airport security. I observed in my own travels how necessary security precautions restricted traveling with beauty products like nail scissors and certain tweezers, which airport security often did not allow on planes. As a result, I suggested that we consider creating an airport-friendly kit of beauty tools approved by the Transportation Security Authority. Leaders must be aware of the world beyond the four walls of their workplace in order to create opportunities.

Employees who open their minds to ideas outside the office are extremely valuable to your organization and add new dimensions to strategy and tactics. Such people are also often up to date on ever-changing trends in your industry or the latest advances in technology.

A few years after I joined Revlon, I decided to search for someone new to lead our sales and customer marketing organization. We needed a team that could think differently about ways to grow our business with our retail customers. I wanted us to be able to dive deep into the details of our business and do a lot of observation and fact finding. It was also necessary for us to have a good grasp of what drove beauty business in our retailers' stores.

When we had a new team established, a team member asked why, in contrast to other retail categories, Revlon beauty products did not enjoy a seasonal boost in sales. With their understanding of mass-market merchandisers, they knew that a disproportionate amount of business normally occurs during the late fall and continues through the end-of-year holiday period. They wondered why Revlon did not see a sales increase during the holidays and benefit from the increased flow of traffic that most retailers recognize—and capitalize on—in other parts of their stores. How could Revlon work to increase its own marketing pressure and improve its approach to these busy promotional periods?

The team suggested marketing programs that would help us benefit from this seasonal pattern. It was simply their curiosity—their willingness to ask questions and work to understand sales data and patterns—that pointed them to examine opportunities to grow our business aggressively.

Look for people who are curious and have a willingness to learn; they will find new ways to add value to your business.

See Opportunities

Have you ever wondered what defines "creative" people? I believe creative people are always receptive to new information. Creative people observe information, facts, events, and ideas—even those that are seemingly unrelated—from different sources and connect them, coming up with innovative solutions. They recognize where there's opportunity for a new brand or line of business, a novel marketing approach, or a new cost-reducing action. They recognize when an administrative procedure could be improved or eliminated. Consider this example:

After being at Revlon for a little more than a year, I was fortunate to hire a man named Carl Kooyoomjian to lead our manufacturing and distribution functions. Carl had managed some of Digital Equipment Corporation's manufacturing functions, and at one time he had been responsible for manufacturing at Coca-Cola.

At about the same time, Revlon was also fortunate to hire Stephanie Peponis, a partner from The Boston Consulting Group. Stephanie led a team of consultants doing strategy work at Revlon. Initially our chief planning officer, she later became our chief marketing officer.

Carl and Stephanie believed that Revlon had done a very good job in the past of reducing the cost of goods, but noted that the manufacturing divisions had instigated most of the previous cost cutting. There had not been an effort to **look for other opportunities to reduce costs across the organization.**

One way was to encourage manufacturing personnel to work closely with marketing, sales, and other company functions. Carl and Stephanie immediately saw an opportunity to create greater cost efficiencies by working more effectively *across* the organization, rather than simply up and down in a single functional area like manufacturing or marketing.

They first observed that if decisions about packaging were made earlier and more cooperatively between our marketing, sales, creative, and production functions, they could improve our cost structure. Accelerating the timing of marketing decisions might give manufacturing more opportunities to reduce production costs *before* the packages and products were introduced to the marketplace. They also recognized that operations people, working with marketing and creative staff to reduce the number of packaging options and components, could streamline our manufacturing process. We could achieve economies of scale through using fewer packages, thereby reducing our cost of goods.

Through great cross-functional work, we uncovered an opportunity to streamline our packaging strategy in a way that would actually decrease costs while enhancing the look and feel of the packaging for our consumers. That overall positive impact helped grow the business while simultaneously reducing our costs by millions of dollars.

It was not Stephanie and Carl's functional knowledge alone that did the trick. Both had excellent communication and team-building skills. Each had the ability to see an opportunity, and both understood the advantage of looking outward, across the organization, for new ways to save costs and move us toward our destination.

Another example of the importance of recognizing opportunities comes from my early days at Coca-Cola. When the Berlin Wall came down in 1989, The Coca-Cola Company had to decide quickly how to build its business in Eastern Germany. I was chief financial officer at the time, and I toured Eastern Germany on a bus for a week along with other senior leaders of Coca-Cola. We saw that there were a huge number of potential Coca-Cola drinkers in Eastern Germany, many of whom had never tasted Coke. The leadership of our company quickly made the major business and financial decision to invest hundreds of millions of dollars to build bottling plants in Eastern Germany.

However, perhaps our company's most significant decision was to accept initially East German currency for the products we sold, rather than accepting only U.S. dollars. This was based on a fast analysis of how we believed the economies in East and West Germany were ultimately likely to converge. That economic convergence would allow the company to realize a healthy return on its investment. This sizable investment would ultimately prove to be an important contributor to the company's long-term growth, and it was based on Coca-Cola people seeing an opportunity that stemmed from new facts, new data, some creative insight into the future, and how that could be turned to the company's advantage.

Find and encourage people to look constantly for new ways to enhance your results and capabilities.

Develop a Detailed Plan and Organize the Necessary Resources for Action

Every organization needs people who can analyze, plan, and communicate what actions and resources are required, who will be responsible, and by when. Not everyone is good at building project plans and determining necessary resources and deadlines; people who can do so are essential for your staff.

Execute a Plan and Focus On the Details

Perhaps the most essential skill an organization needs from its employees is **the ability to get things done.** There is no substitute for people who are willing and able to handle details, produce timely results, and do it under pressure and in a variety of environments.

As a leader, it is important that you focus on quality execution—the ability to see problems early, develop alternative solutions, and then take all necessary actions to resolve the problem as soon as possible. For example, good execution skills require the ability to seek out and identify any indications of potential slip-ups in product quality or customer service.

The next step should be to dispatch the right people to fix these problems, however small the issues might seem initially. Like the saying goes, the movement of a few snowflakes can bring on an avalanche. By personally communicating your commitment to developing these important execution skills and practices throughout the organization, and attracting people who think that way, your company can avoid significant problems, which might be more difficult and costly to solve if allowed to grow through inattention.

Key Point

There is no substitute for people who are willing and able to complete effectively both detailed "grunt" work and "high-level" work in a timely way, and in different environments.

Effectively Communicate and Work as Part of a Team

Teamwork ensures that the people and departments involved with a project are all focused on the same objectives, each understanding what the other is doing to achieve them, and helping each other to get things done on time. When someone presents a proposal to me, I often ask if they have reviewed the proposal with other relevant departments. That way, people know they are expected to get input from others early on. This is necessary to improve their view of the project as a whole and to avoid unnecessary problems that might limit its success. Here's an example of how successful teamwork on a project can achieve a major organizational objective:

I mentioned the strategy to turn a large Coca-Cola bottler into a publicly held company. To do this, I worked with a group of people to execute the very sizeable public stock offering of Coca-Cola Enterprises, a large Coca-Cola bottler. This equity offering raised $1 billion. A team of about 15 of us, all considered capable performers with good skills, executed it. We represented different departments of the company, such as finance, treasury, tax, accounting, legal, human resources, operations, marketing, sales, and public relations. The project involved accomplishing many major subordinate projects on deadline. Each activity, from developing the pro-forma financial statements of the company to developing a prospectus describing the operations of the new company; from involving investment bankers to develop a public offering strategy, to focusing on the detailed mechanics of setting up the new public company; from completing the acquisition of operations to be included in the new company all the way through to finding physical space for the new entity—everything had to be closely studied, planned, and executed.

I was the day-to-day leader of this working group. Given the complexity of the project, from the beginning it was obvious to all of us the importance of excellent communication and teamwork. Our team met weekly to review progress against each element of the work plan, and in the process we worked very effectively as a team. Each team-member called out his or her responsibilities and updated the group on progress. We worked very hard to recognize and address issues and challenges. Each of us was willing to call out where we were struggling to get something done and where we needed help or advice. We provided that advice to each other. When we saw something not getting done as planned, we asked why; then we offered feedback and solutions in a constructive way.

Every group member clearly understood the power of being candid and sharing with each other. As a result, no member was ever put in a position to be out-negotiated by someone outside our company because of a communication failure within the team. That generated a tremendous amount of confidence. Good teamwork and an excellent plan gave us the conviction that we could overcome any barrier to get the job done. It became clear that the **tighter and more detailed our**

intercommunication became, the more effective we became. Toward the end of the project, we delighted in announcing to each other our successes and accomplishments. We measured and charted our progress in moving toward the successful completion of the offering that would form the large, publicly held Coca-Cola Enterprises.

Moreover, we did just that, completing the public offering in the course of 100 days, an astoundingly short period for such a large public offering. This effective, timely, and successful execution of a complex plan was also a huge learning experience for each of us about the importance of being a good team player and the power of strong teams. In addition, we also gained amazing cross-functional insights and honed our core skills while doing it.

As you build your organization, look for and reward those people who work effectively as part of teams; they will be important to your success.

Recognize and Develop the Skills of Others

People are the most costly investment of many organizations and drive its greatest returns. Giving good coaching and timely feedback will develop strong performers who will bring your organization the highest return on its investment.

I always practiced this skill when I had the opportunity. I was very fortunate at Revlon to have had an assistant named Ange Justice. Ange had excellent administrative skills and the ability to manage my often-changing schedule and effectively represent my office to people within and outside Revlon. She's very proud—as am I—of the results of this next example, which demonstrates the importance of this sixth core skill.

At the time, we had instituted a program to teach 6,000 Revlon employees core communication and coaching skills, so that each employee could communicate more effectively with his or her coworkers and customers. We decided to use a "train the trainer" approach. Approximately 60 Revlon people would be selected and trained to instruct all the remaining people at Revlon. I believed that Ange would be an exceptional trainer, and I asked her if she'd like to apply.

She was very surprised. As an assistant, she didn't expect to be selected as a trainer. I encouraged her to see this as an opportunity to further her own development. Although at first she was skeptical, Ange accepted the challenge and did a terrific job. She became a successful trainer, honing important core skills in doing it.

Soon, that new skill brought Ange another opportunity when someone commented that the train-the-trainer program was a prime example of a Revlon success story. We decided it would be great to share the "nuts and bolts" of the program with other people in the company. Several people asked me to suggest to Ange that she make a 15-minute presentation at an upcoming company event about her experiences as a trainer. At first, she declined—she had a vacation scheduled that week.

I told Ange that it would be important to many other employees at Revlon if she made the speech. Moreover, it would be personally rewarding for her—speaking in front of a large group of several hundred people would develop her presentation skills.

Ange looked me in the eye and said, "Jack, I told you I wanted to develop my skills, but I never told you I wanted to develop them in front of 400 people at once!"

We both laughed, and I figured that was the end of it, but Ange had taken what I said to heart. She thought it over, and changed her mind.

She changed her vacation plans, prepared her speech, and did an outstanding job of presenting her story to our people. Ange handled her presentation as though she had been speaking to large groups for her entire career. She received wonderful feedback from folks everywhere in the organization about how important her work as a trainer had been to them.

Leadership Insight

Ultimately, your objective should be to make your people even more effective than you, their leader, are.

Ange's success also sent a message around the company that we could successfully move people into new and challenging projects and roles when they were properly prepared, and they could have a positive impact on the organization, far beyond what was expected. The ongoing health of any organization depends on its dedication to helping employees increase their skills. A leader must believe that developing people is of paramount importance because it allows the organization to succeed, grow, and achieve its objectives. Leaders need to provide quality feedback to employees—about their performance, skills, and future growth opportunities—in a constructive way. The difference in contribution and output between a strong performer and a weak performer is dramatic. In addition, a high rate of turnover and loss of critical talent is costly in the long run to any organization.

Key Point

Grow the capabilities of your organization by ensuring that you have managers who can attract and develop strong people.

As part of your overall people development approach, when considering an employee's next assignment, think about the skills he or she will bring into the assignment, as well as the skills the new job would require him or her to develop. My experience has shown me that most individuals in a new position can learn only a few new skills at a time. In addition, be aware that you may ask too much if you require someone to learn new skills as he or she adjusts and adapts to an unfamiliar geographic location or culture.

Author Alvin Toffler called this effect *future shock,* "the shattering stress and disorientation we induce in individuals by subjecting them to too much change in too short a time."

After more than three decades of technological advances and a shifting global economy, people have adapted to quantum leaps of change in a very short time. Even so, rapid changes remain a stress-producing element of business life. If you have to put someone in this kind of situation, understand the extreme pressures it creates and be prepared to invest a lot of personal time to provide direction and support during the adjustment period.

Key Question to Consider

Do your employees clearly understand what skills and performance will determine their success within your organization? If not, people may perceive that favoritism and politics determine success, and, as a result, they may not commit to their own development and the organization's success.

RECRUIT AND ASSIGN JOBS BASED ON THE NECESSARY SKILLS TO SUCCEED

There are many models for successful recruiting. Examine yours carefully to determine that it's the right model for your company's destination.

The interview process is one of the most vital steps in creating a high-capability organization. When conducting interviews, I suggest that you ask for *very specific* examples of past success directly relating to the skills required by the assignment under consideration. If you can't elicit concrete examples of the candidate using the core skills to create positive results, he or she probably isn't the employee you're seeking.

> ### Key Point
> *Participate in the interview process for critical roles.*

Several years ago, I was looking for someone to fill the senior financial role at Revlon. One of the skills we were looking for was the ability to build a financial organization that could effectively relate to its business counterparts in order to provide appropriate financial service, support, and controls. I wanted someone with the right financial management skills, but who also knew how to create a team to make effective connections with marketing, manufacturing, sales, and legal.

I asked the first candidate whom I interviewed to provide specific examples of how in the past he had approached building a financial organization to provide this kind of support. He focused his response solely on how he had *personally* interacted with his cross-functional counterparts and built one-on-one relationships. He did not demonstrate that he had ever built the kind of strong financial *team* I was looking for. His answer indicated that he did not have the skills to build the financial organization we needed at Revlon.

Key Point

Require that interviewees give you very specific examples of when, where, and how they have demonstrated the behaviors and actions required for success in the potential new assignment.

In contrast, the second candidate, Tom McGuire (who we ultimately hired) provided me with *specific* examples of his previous experience in building a financial organization. He detailed explicitly how, in a previous position, he had started by attracting five or six analytically oriented financial people with a mix of good accounting, financial analysis, and communication skills. He had then used those people to build relationships with *their* cross-functional counterparts, positioning them to provide accounting, financial analysis, and project management support. After awhile, these five or six people were in position to provide exceptional financial service and strong financial controls.

Tom also emphasized that these people had served as the "front end" of the financial organization, which allowed him to continue to rely on his more experienced staff to provide the appropriate financial support in the areas of accounts receivable, accounts payable, financial accounting, and information systems. Those functional areas of finance were able to continue to do their jobs effectively, while the new people he brought into the organization were tasked with reaching out across the organization to their cross-functional counterparts. That built out and increased the financial division's services and sphere of influence, all of which helped to move the business forward.

When I interviewed him, by describing *specifically* the actions he had taken in the past, Tom gave me confidence that he could play the role we needed. Tom did a terrific job as chief financial officer at Revlon and ultimately went on to run the company's international business.

It is also important to know when someone simply does not have the ability or interest to develop skills in a particular area. It is pointless to try to force square pegs into round holes in personnel management. Avoid putting people into roles in which they have no interest or potential. It is far better to let a person in this situation focus on his or her strengths. In larger organizations, there are positions that require people with strong technical skills who may be uninterested in managing or training others. Some technical performers prefer to remain individual contributors. Capitalize on the strong technical ability of those people and do not push them to manage others. It doesn't work.

The best job assignments allow people to utilize existing strengths and skills they can demonstrate with clear examples of past experience, while giving them the opportunity to learn and acquire new skills in the new role.

Leadership Insight

Recruiting and staffing need not be a hit-or-miss process. There is a logical approach to putting the right people into the right roles.

Key Questions to Consider

Are your hiring managers (with support from your human resources team) able to clearly define and communicate the core skills necessary for success in your organization to those who will be recruiting and interviewing candidates to fill those needs? When setting up an interview schedule for a candidate, take the time to decide what core skills are important for the role. Design interview questions that seek examples of when and how the candidate displayed those skills in the past and with what results. Divide up these questions among the various interviewers. This will allow you to get a much better read on the candidate's capabilities for the job and the candidate will be given a thorough opportunity to highlight the experiences that are most relevant.

Are you relying on "soft" information, or unclear communication, when interviewing a potential employee? Ask follow-up questions to get precise answers to your questions!

INVEST IN AND CAPITALIZE ON DIVERSITY

Businesses benefit from diversity. If managed effectively, people from different backgrounds, cultures, and experiences can contribute a wide variety of solutions. There is no finer example I can offer than Coca-Cola CEO Roberto Goizueta, who fled his native Cuba in 1954 with little more than a suitcase and his education as a chemical engineer. He eventually rose to become head of The Coca-Cola Company, one of the biggest, most successful, and enduring American companies. Based on his background and experience working in many countries and cultures, as well as his intelligence and personality, Mr. Goizueta brought tremendous perspective and capability to his role as CEO. He believed in diversity at Coca-Cola, and he actively promoted it.

"Perhaps no other corporate leader in modern times has so beautifully exemplified the American dream," said former President

Jimmy Carter when he learned of Roberto Goizueta's death in 1997. "He believed that, in America, all things are possible. He lived that dream."

Leadership Insight

Success is often the result of different ideas arising from different perspectives. Seek out—and capitalize on—a diverse workforce.

Goizueta knew that our business depended on working successfully with customers, consumers, and employees in more than 180 countries who spoke many languages and came from many cultures. In the mid-1990s we began a broad program to increase our ability to interact effectively with a global marketplace. We defined diversity as the differences among people surrounding language, culture, ways of thinking and approaching problems, work and life experiences, religion, personal style, and any other important differences among people. We set out to learn how to make these differences become strengths in solving problems and creating opportunities. We created training programs in which employees were videotaped in order to view our own behaviors in familiar and then unfamiliar environments. Then we watched the tapes to learn how we were effective and when we were not. This exercise helped us understand our own "default" behaviors. Roberto Goizueta proved that it is *profitable* for an organization to seek and capitalize on a workforce that reflects and complements the diverse needs of your business. By doing so, you gain better insights into the wide spectrum of cultural influences, needs, and preferences of your customers and consumers.

A diverse workforce is part of being a capable organization, one that will drive stronger results for shareowners.

Key Question to Consider

Are you investing strongly in diversity? Commit yourself and your top executives to developing and attracting a diverse workforce. Be sure your human resources people, and your senior managers, are committed to that goal and that they develop strategies to attract and hire a wide range of capable people across your organization at all levels. They will bring you varied viewpoints, and valuable ideas and solutions. Build a critical mass of diverse talent and thinking that will become self-sustaining, and can continue to build upon itself. Understand that this process requires a significant personal effort from you, as the leader, and you must dedicate the effort and resources that will be required to accomplish it.

CLOSING STATEMENT

My own experience constantly reminds me that even the most capable leaders cannot create great results without outstanding people who 1) understand the overall direction of the organization, 2) have the skills necessary to create success, and 3) are motivated and committed to achieving that success.

If you are diligent in setting a path for your organization and committing the energy to attract and develop the people who will enable success, I believe you will have taken the first important step in moving toward creating the results you desire.

Developing
People

The third framework is perhaps my favorite because it relates to developing people, the most enjoyable part of my business experience.

After I earned my MBA at Wharton and accepted a job at the accounting firm Arthur Andersen LLP, I learned first-hand that skillful employees are absolutely critical to an organization's success. I worked as an auditor and management consultant, which from the outset gave me terrific cross-functional exposure to manufacturing, finance, and other areas of business. On one assignment, I saw how the accounting and financial analysis teams completed the year-end financial closing process. Each member of the team understood the technical aspects of his or her job and communicated effectively with other team members. As a result, the closing process was completed seamlessly, in a cost-efficient manner, and under tight time constraints. The experience taught me the importance of skilled people working together as a team across all business functions of a company, to create positive results. That early understanding has served me extremely well as I have moved along in my career.

I left Arthur Andersen in 1979 and accepted a position with The Coca-Cola Company. My first job at Coca-Cola was to represent the company to the investment community, communicating our financial results, strategies for growth, and progress to strengthen the company. To succeed, I depended on colleagues throughout Coca-Cola to provide the insights and information that I needed to communicate the company's progress. While the company was introducing Diet Coke to the investment community during the early 1980s, I met extensively with the marketing team responsible for the project. I came to understand the depth of analysis, strategic thinking, and detailed planning that went into identifying a major new product opportunity and planning for its launch. I had the chance to observe the marketing team working with Coca-Cola bottlers, who were responsible for producing and distributing the new product on a very tight timeline. The process of preparing for the launch required very skilled work and effective communication among marketing, research and development, manufacturing, finance, and public relations. That launch was very successful and generated significant profits for The Coca-Cola Company and Coca-Cola bottlers.

These early experiences working with capable people—and the skills I gained from them—ultimately shaped my thinking about the importance of developing people to an organization's success and growth. As a young leader, I recognized that only with teamwork that combined each employee's skills could we maximize the power of our brands and create outstanding results for The Coca-Cola Company. I also learned that creating results like these required people having the core skills I described in the previous framework. These core skills help enable people to capitalize on the inherent strengths they bring to a role as a result of their background, experiences, and personality.

There are many different models for people development. The one I believe to be most effective calls for defining and communicating the core skills that are necessary for success and ensuring that people are provided with good feedback and coaching about these skills. Ideally, people will learn them in both existing and then new, challenging roles in different departments, because the core skills apply, and often can be learned best, by working in different functional areas during the course of your career. By using this approach, leaders maximize their employees' contributions to an organization, as well as their options for career growth by not limiting their development to a single professional area.

Encouraging employees to learn the core skills early on and practice them through increasingly challenging roles and assignments brought the results that we worked for at Coca-Cola as individuals, a team, and as a company. My greatest satisfaction came from helping others maximize the potential of the company through the acquisition of these core skills and seeing them understand, over time, that they were also maximizing their *own* potential by doing that. I hope that this framework will also help you determine what additional skills are important to you and your business, and show you how to proceed in modeling, teaching, and reinforcing those skills.

Developing people continues to inspire, excite, and challenge me. I know that I will continue to enjoy it after my career at Revlon, whether I accept a leadership position inside another corporation, or if I choose to consult in the area of people and organizational development. I hope that sharing my experiences here will help you build and capture that same kind of excitement and reward.

DRIVE THE PROCESS OF DEVELOPING PEOPLE

I realized early in my career that the difference in contribution and output between a strong performer and a weak performer is dramatic. **The most effective leaders focus tremendous energy on hiring and supporting strong performers, in order to build the team they need to achieve organizational goals.** The people who work to create success must share it. They also deserve your help to support the building of their skills in order to become strong performers motivated to create future successes. You will need to devote time to interact directly with them to show that you value their success and are personally willing to help them achieve it. Believe me when I say that spending significant development time with your people will be extremely worthwhile to them and your organization's bottom line.

There are seven basic techniques for leaders that I believe are critical to successful people development. You'd be amazed at how few organizational leaders have grasped these simple but critical techniques.

1. Comprehend the difference between "core skills" and "exposure."
2. Create opportunities for both "project" and "process" experience.
3. Use an effective model for feedback and appraisals.
4. Utilize control systems as development tools.
5. Be situational in your management style.
6. Manage compensation strategically.
7. Use mistakes strategically.

From these techniques and insights, you can easily adapt an approach to developing the skills of your people that is specific to the needs of your organization and your leadership situation.

COMPREHEND THE DIFFERENCE BETWEEN CORE SKILLS AND EXPOSURE

Many people believe that *exposure* to various functions, cultures, and work environments is important to career growth. I agree. Yet, I have met many people with a broad and varied work experience who never acquired the core skills necessary for career success. Despite the breadth of their experience, these people were eventually "exposed" when they were unable to achieve great results.

I cannot emphasize enough how necessary it is for you to *coach the people you believe have strong potential for your organization,* encouraging them early in their careers to seek a variety of jobs and projects, where they have the opportunity and enough time in each role to learn the core skills that will be critical to achieving success throughout their careers. Be sure they'll work with others, in other organizational functions, who will help them develop. As they progress to different assignments, their supervisors should be capable of teaching them these core skills, through effective feedback and coaching.

One colleague at Coca-Cola, who I'll call "George," was a longtime manager-level employee who had not learned these critical skills early in his career. Unfortunately, he was not as effective as he could have been—or as the company needed him to be. George had just applied for an international assignment in Germany, and I had asked him to come and talk to me about it. In the meantime, I had reviewed his evaluations from past assignments and saw that he was lacking in execution skills—he was not getting projects done on time.

George settled himself into the chair in my office, and I asked him why he wanted to transfer to Germany.

He said, "I've been here in the U.S. business for a long time, Jack, and I want to broaden my focus. I've always wanted to live in Europe, and I'm looking forward to that, and the changes this assignment will bring. I think I have the right background and experience for this position."

"This will be a whole new working and living environment for you, George," I commented. "Do you speak German?"

"No," he admitted, "but I figure I can take lessons and learn it pretty quickly. I'm looking forward to working in an international environment. It will give me broader perspective and exposure, and that should really be positive for my career."

It was obvious from his enthusiasm that he was very anxious to make this job and location change. Yet, I also knew that he was often unable to execute important projects, which his new position would require. He lacked the attention to detail required to get things done the way they should be done. I also suspected George was taking the easy way out by choosing not to focus on his development areas. I tried to lead him in another direction.

"You're absolutely right, George, different assignments and exposure could be important to your ultimate success with the company. But I think it's more important for your career right now that you stay put, George. I think we should focus attention on you getting coaching to acquire better execution skills, before tackling a new assignment in a whole new culture, with a different language."

After that comment, I leafed through his file, giving him time to absorb my comments.

George knew that I was familiar with his evaluations and his supervisors' feedback. He shifted in his chair a bit, realizing this wasn't going to be an easy conversation. Then he acknowledged the problem.

"There's no reason I can't work on my execution skills over there, as well as here," George said. "I really want this position in Germany, Jack. For one thing, it's available now, and may not be later."

"That's true," I agreed, and sat back in my chair, encouraging him to relax. "But there will be other international assignments that will open up, George, probably in Germany as well as other areas. My concern is that if you go to Germany right now, and plunge into a new job and new culture, your whole focus will be on adapting to that language and culture, as well as the demands of this new position. That won't leave you the time you'll need to focus on gaining better execution skills. You may end up putting it off, and that will limit your career success, even with the international exposure. I'm suggesting that you stay here, and if you do, I'll personally help you improve your execution skills. Then you can seek an international position."

Nevertheless, I was unable to convince George that he was making a strategic career mistake.

George went to Germany, and he later transferred to Asia for even more international exposure. As predicted, he never did focus on or get coaching to improve his execution skills, and therefore he never reached his career potential. Eventually, he was asked to leave Coca-Cola.

Was George's lack of execution skills completely his fault? Probably not—the company had not placed the required emphasis on teaching him those skills earlier in his career. Reflecting on this, I knew that we needed to clearly define the core skills that were required for success in our organization, and be diligent in communicating a picture of success to our employees that included those skills. We also needed to ensure that employees received the kind of timely and consistent training, coaching, and feedback that acquiring and improving the critical skills required.

At Coca-Cola, we did so with great success, and later we built training, performance feedback systems, and job assignments around them.

Later, when I joined Revlon, the human resources division defined, communicated, and put processes in place to develop the important and relevant skills. Two of the core skills that we judged to be most important were communication and how to provide performance feedback to other employees. We trained hundreds of people in these areas and, without a doubt, the improvement in those two skills alone helped enhance the company's performance.

CREATE OPPORTUNITIES FOR BOTH PROJECT AND PROCESS EXPERIENCE

Give people the opportunity to work on major projects that have a beginning and end date, projects that you expect to produce a specific set of results and outcomes. This kind of experience forces people to learn to perform a series of specific actions:

- Creating a plan
- Finding and acquiring necessary resources
- Adhering to deadlines
- Utilizing close cross-functional communication
- Working under pressure

The Coca-Cola bottler public offering that I mentioned earlier was one part of the company's ongoing strategy of consolidating and strengthening the Coca-Cola bottling system. It gave the project's management team the opportunity to experience and learn every element of the project management skills listed above. This billion-dollar project, as described earlier in Framework 2, involved acquiring a number of Coca-Cola bottlers, combining them into a newly formed company, issuing common stock, and listing the new company, Coca-Cola Enterprises, on the New York Stock Exchange.

In order to successfully manage this project, our team put together a detailed work plan that called out by date every key step of the project. This required input from people in finance, legal, tax, and other areas of the company. Once we had a plan in place, we scoped out what personnel would be required and estimated those costs. Then we had to secure people that could commit their time for the next three months. With the plan and necessary resources in place, we began the process of acquiring the Coca-Cola bottlers to be included in the new company, which required our team's careful coordination of deadlines for each acquisition. We set up weekly meetings to review progress compared to our planned timelines. Often in these meetings, we would find something off track, and we could then react immediately to solve a potential problem before it jeopardized the whole project. Here, I learned the importance of frequent communication, especially across departments. For example, if our human resources team member identified an unusually costly employee benefit plan in one of the companies we were acquiring, we immediately asked our financial staff to evaluate the ongoing cost of this benefit program. We could then factor this analysis into our negotiations with the seller.

I'm proud to say that because we created and managed effectively against a detailed plan with the right resources, we were able to work well under pressure to complete the overall project successfully. We met the deadlines for acquiring the bottlers that would help form the new company, issued new stock, listed the company on the New York Stock Exchange, and ultimately saw it begin to operate in the soft drink marketplace effectively.

Key Point

An important oversight technique for major projects is to schedule frequent project updates, and be sure that when someone says something is done, it is totally complete.

Here are key elements of the day-to-day management of the project:

- In our routine update meetings, we reviewed the status of each planned key "action step" from each and every functional area.

- As the project progressed, we made sure that when a team member said something was done, it was *totally complete* with no remaining action required.

- We worked to be very precise in our communication to avoid any confusion or misunderstanding.

- At least once during each project update meeting, we focused on each team member and asked him or her to explain any problems or issues that needed to be reported to the group. By doing so, we could direct attention to those problem areas after the meeting.

- We paid very close attention to details, however insignificant.

- Following each meeting, the project coordinator compiled and sent out a "to do" list to the project team members in each department, indicating who was responsible for accomplishing what and by when.

- Between meetings, the project leader followed up on the status of key pending items to ensure appropriate actions were being taken.

I had the opportunity to manage that project early in my career, at age 33. Working with a team comprised of staff from different divisions and bringing them together routinely helped me develop the core skills I would need to progress into more challenging levels of leadership. The experience reinforced the importance of providing project management assignments to young leaders.

Beyond project roles, most jobs in organizations have routine *processes*. This means that on any given day, people receive information, analyze it, make decisions, and then take action. Most managerial and leadership roles also will require heavy process orientation, in addition to some project management activity.

Leadership Insight

Working against intense deadlines creates pressure that, if managed effectively, can contribute to personal growth.

For that reason, experience in areas that have the same daily routine—such as a customer service unit or the accounts payable department—can provide valuable skill-gaining experience early on in a person's career. These process jobs may not appear creative, challenging, or fun, but they are critical activities offering important learning experiences. They also force one to focus on details and discover what is necessary to successfully manage a process. Hands-on experience in both project and process management is an asset for effective leadership later on.

Key Question to Consider

Does your organization have a way for its cross-functional leadership to discuss open job positions and to surface potential candidates from across the organization to fill them? You might want to consider setting up a "Career Development Committee," where cross-functional leaders meet to discuss what skills are important for certain jobs and then determine which employees across the organization may have the skills to fill these positions when the jobs open up. By doing so, people in your organization will gain confidence knowing that they will be considered for jobs for which they are qualified outside of their immediate department.

Leadership Insight

Core skills translate across most departments and organizations.

USE AN EFFECTIVE MODEL FOR FEEDBACK
AND APPRAISALS

When you speak to your personnel about their skills and performance, consider using the following six-step feedback and coaching model that I utilized. I have found it to be very effective, and there's nothing complicated or difficult about learning to use it.

1. Value the individual and his or her strengths and contributions.

2. Ask the person to assess his or her own performance and discuss where he or she is encountering the greatest challenges in the job.

3. Provide clear and pointed feedback relative to the critical skill or area of performance where you want to see improvement.

4. Agree on the areas of focus and skill development for the future.

5. Agree on the benefits of improving and the consequences of not improving certain skills.

6. Commit your support for and reiterate the value of the individual.

Value the individual. Let the person know that you value him or her as an individual, as well as a contributor to the organization, by discussing the employee's specific strengths and contributions.

Ask the person to assess his or her own performance and discuss where he or she is encountering the greatest challenges in the job. Candid feedback and careful coaching are critical to developing strong performers in any organization. Time and time again, I have found that self-assessment revealed critical areas of an employee's development where I could provide specific feedback and coaching.

Provide clear and pointed feedback relative to the critical skill or area of performance where you want to see improvement. Use specific examples from the past to provide feedback on what you have observed. Discuss how a different approach might create a more successful outcome. If a person has identified an area where he or she struggles, get the person to talk about his or her current approach to the area. Then you can discuss it, evaluate other approaches, and perhaps discover an opportunity for further training.

Agree on the areas of focus and skill development for the future. Find projects or assignments for the person you are coaching that offer an opportunity to practice new skills. You may also be able to suggest some targeted training that you think will help him or her overcome areas of frustration.

Agree on the benefits of improving and the consequences of not improving certain skills. Explain the short- or long-term benefits of improving skills and the consequences of not doing so. Ask follow-up questions to be sure the person clearly understands such benefits and consequences.

Commit your support for and reiterate the value of the individual. Reinforce positive comments about the person's personal strengths and reemphasize his or her importance to your organization so that the employee departs on a positive note and feels motivated to take the agreed-upon skill-building steps.

I strongly encourage you to try this six-step appraisal and feedback model, even if you have to do it mechanically at first. It will become easier and more relaxed for you with practice. I think you'll be surprised by the results.

I used this model effectively during an appraisal session with "Jennifer," who admitted that she was having difficulty influencing "Mike," a colleague in her department. I determined that I needed to observe Jennifer and Mike interacting to decide if further coaching could resolve what Jennifer saw as an ongoing challenge to her success.

Mike had a strong personality. I noticed that when Mike interacted with Jennifer, he would stake out an extreme position. He could be fairly provocative, and he was able to pull people over to his side with his forceful opinions, which was sometimes not the best outcome for the organization.

Because she was unable to influence him, I decided to have a coaching session with Jennifer, emphasizing communication and influencing skills. I asked her what she thought had taken place at the meeting that I had observed, and her reply was consistent with what I saw.

"I thought Mike took a pretty extreme position on the point we were discussing," she said. "To react to that, I think I probably took an equally extreme opposite position, which didn't get me anywhere."

I asked, "What if you go back and reopen the issue you and Mike just discussed? But, rather than taking the opposite position, how about taking the middle ground for yourself? In the conversation, set yourself on ground you can defend, support, and feel comfortable standing firm on. Since it's a reasonable place to be, maybe it will work better for you in influencing someone like Mike. "

Jennifer said she'd give it a try.

I made sure I was there when they met again. Jennifer staked out the middle ground for herself and stood resolute while she listened to Mike's extreme position. Soon, in the course of the debate, it became clear to Mike that Jennifer was steadfast. He also realized that she had taken a reasonable and well-grounded position and the others in that meeting were beginning to gravitate to her point of view. Ultimately, Mike tired of supporting what I think he instinctively knew was an unreasonable position. Jennifer was able to bring Mike to a reasonable agreement on middle ground.

It was only when I had asked for her thoughts about her development that Jennifer realized her ineffective approach to influencing Mike. Today, Jennifer is a stronger communicator and effectively influences others because she takes positions that are solidly grounded in facts. Our conversation and the coaching I gave her based on this model for feedback and appraisals not only helped her to develop, but it also helped Mike. After that, he more frequently took reasonable positions during discussions.

Key Questions to Consider

Are you being consistent in the feedback that you provide an individual about your expectations? It is reassuring when employees get consistency from their boss and disorienting when they don't.

Are you dealing with development issues immediately? If you are not dealing with development issues immediately then you are not only missing an opportunity to help maximize a person's potential, but you are also creating bigger problems for your organization and the employee down the road.

UTILIZE CONTROL SYSTEMS AS DEVELOPMENT TOOLS

One element of effective control systems is to require management to approve certain actions. Then you can use discussions during the approval process to:

- Create opportunities for joint learning.
- Allow the discovery of new facts and insights.
- Assist in the continued development of people.

When I became controller of The Coca-Cola Company in 1988, I suggested to my boss, Doug Ivester (then our CFO), that I should personally be able to approve financial decisions of up to $10 million. Mr. Ivester disagreed and told me my limit would be $1 million, not $10 million. Why?

He knew that by limiting the actions I could approve personally, he would retain more control when I was new to my job. He also knew that the lower approval limit meant I'd initiate more discussions with him about financial decisions in order to get him to sign off. That would create more opportunities for him to coach me. As I acquired more knowledge and increased my skills, Mr. Ivester became confident in my abilities. Soon, he elevated my approval levels. Mr. Ivester was effectively utilizing control systems as developmental tools, just as you can.

BE SITUATIONAL IN YOUR MANAGEMENT STYLE

There are times when a new employee needs to be closely managed and supervised. Yet, as employees develop, managers ought to step back as they offer support, coaching, and encouragement.

I was managed differently at different points in my career. One of my most important early learning experiences at Coca-Cola was the sale by the company of a non soft drink business. Mr. Ivester called me often, sometimes asking where we were in the status of negotiations on something or returning one of my calls asking him for advice on our next move.

On one occasion, I called Mr. Ivester around 11:30 p.m. We were trying to close the deal before year end, and the deadline was close. The potential buyer for this $100-million business was trying to delay in order to extract further negotiating concessions. He knew that he would be at an advantage if The Coca-Cola Company had to hurry to make a deal at the year-end deadline. I had called Mr. Ivester to explain the buyer's tactics. When he returned my call, Mr. Ivester did something very important to me at that point. He demonstrated his confidence in the job I was doing, and at the same time he reinforced my position in the negotiations.

He said, "Jack, you've been working this deal now for three months—you've been close to it. I've been giving you some guidance, but you're the person on the ground. I can't tell you what to do here, but what I can tell you is, no one should be allowed to take advantage of you and The Coca-Cola Company."

Mr. Ivester sent a clear signal that he didn't want me to feel unfair pressure to get the transaction done by year end. I had his support and the company's backing. His call assured me of his confidence in my judgment and my ability to get the deal done, and done right.

I went back to the buyer and resumed negotiating from a stronger position. We completed the deal successfully, and it closed before year end. Our success was gratifying and it built my confidence in my ability to complete a significant business negotiation.

Leadership Insight

Development occurs through frequent problem-solving and coaching conversations with experienced and skilled leaders in an organization.

Early in the negotiations, Mr. Ivester had been very involved in the details. He used the right mix of close direction and attention to detail. Later, he backed off and offered mainly emotional support as the transaction progressed and my knowledge and confidence grew. That allowed a big leap forward in my negotiation and project management skills. Mr. Ivester was very situational and perceptive as a leader. Your ability to assess and adapt to evolving situations may also be key to maximizing an employee's strengths and success.

When I was newly assigned to The Coca-Cola Company's mergers and acquisitions group, I had virtually no experience in that area. Doug Ivester understood my need for coaching and close direction at the outset. We sometimes spoke five or six times each day. Once I became controller, I had 11 years of finance experience with Coca-Cola. Mr. Ivester and I spoke only two or three times each month. He continued to be situational in his management style.

When I began as CEO and president of Revlon in 2002, chairman Ronald Perelman was very involved in the details at first. At the time, he focused on the analytics of the business. Sometimes he'd have ten or 15 questions for me each day, all of which necessitated that I delve deeply into numbers and details. Doing so helped me to understand a new business—the cosmetics and beauty-care industry—faster than I might have otherwise. By virtue of his keen interest and incisive questions, he helped me to quickly focus on what I needed to learn right away.

As Mr. Perelman became confident that I was familiar with the business, the direction of our interaction shifted. Our discussions revolved more around overall strategy. The gradual change illustrated Mr. Perelman's ability to be flexible and situational in his leadership.

I also had the pleasure of working with the late Roberto Goizueta when he was CEO and chairman of Coca-Cola. Roberto took the time to evaluate skills and personality traits to ensure that he hired the right people. Roberto understood that if someone took over a job supported by a good infrastructure and staff, then he could accept someone who was initially less familiar with the details of the position. Even without the technical competence the job typically requires, an employee with broad-based core skills could draw upon the existing staff and good coaching to do the job. Roberto didn't micro-manage at a detail level. He relied instead on the executive's experience, knowledge, background, and abilities, while factoring in the support structure already in place for that area or position.

Ivester, Perelman, and Goizueta represent strong examples of excellent and insightful leadership. Although each used different approaches, they all recognized the value of being situational in their leadership and management styles. Each in a different way encouraged and helped me develop my own strengths, skills, and business effectiveness. Doug Ivester managed situationally as my responsibilities evolved and my skills and confidence grew. Ronald Perelman understood the importance of being detailed in his own approach, particularly if someone was new to a situation, and then shifting his attention to broader strategy as my understanding of the industry and the organization grew. Roberto understood how to assess not only the employee, but also the position he or she inherited.

Small businesses can also profit from situational management principles. *Restaurant Business News* magazine described how a restaurant owner allowed student servers to study on his dime. Servers could show up for the dinner shift, pitch in during the busy hours, and then study in the back of the restaurant during downtime even though they were still on the clock. The restaurateur thought it was better to get some of the staff's time, rather than have them call in "sick" on heavy homework nights. Meanwhile, during the slack period, while students caught up on their homework, the rest of the waitstaff got more tables and tips.

Each of the above examples reinforces the importance of leaders being situational in their leadership styles, in order to maximize both the development of people and their impact on results.

Key Question to Consider

Are you focusing enough of your management time on the strong performers in your organization? Managers often spend too much time focusing on "problem" people. You should deal with those who perform poorly—perhaps by moving them out of your organization, if their performance shows little improvement after your coaching. As their leader, you need to spend time with your strong performers to reinforce their strengths and abilities. With leadership attention and consistent feedback, they will grow faster and perform better. Ultimately, they will drive the greatest results for your organization.

MANAGE COMPENSATION STRATEGICALLY

As you consider different approaches to managing compensation, it is important to recognize that **shareholders do not want to pay for unfulfilled potential; they want to pay for results.**

For that reason, if no other, the approach to compensation that makes the most sense is to link a person's rewards to his demonstrated ability to generate positive results and value for the organization. Yet, many organizational compensation models don't work that way.

Changes in compensation and rewards should not occur long before—or after—a person demonstrates the ability to drive positive results. You should match a person's growth in pay to corresponding growth in skills and accomplishments. Because a person's ability to generate results grows gradually, consider giving raises more frequently in smaller increments, rather than a system of infrequent or regularly scheduled larger increases given on an annual review basis.

Many managers choose to give large promotional increases the day a person moves into a new role. I prefer to delay some of that initial "promotion" increase and award it when the individual has been in the job for a while and has created positive results in the new position. People really appreciate such a compensation "kicker" when they have begun to conquer the challenges of their role. It shows that you are **paying attention to that individual's actual performance, rather than a calendar,** and that you appreciate and reward good results.

Key Point

People's ability to generate results usually grows in a gradual fashion, not in big jumps. Reward results and growth in skills.

Rewarding for results and acquired skills, rather than simply for title, position, or calendar date, is an effective way to maximize an individual's growth. Use this compensation management approach to **encourage strong performance and have a positive impact on both the employee and the organization.**

USE MISTAKES STRATEGICALLY

When you place people in roles where they will be required to develop new skills, expect that they will make mistakes; it is part of the learning process. However, you should ensure that your people understand the consequences of mistakes that result from a lack of timeliness or attention to detail. I think the best way to encourage people to avoid repeating errors is to make them work their way out of mistakes on their own—even if the process is somewhat painful.

When employees at Coca-Cola made a mistake, Roberto Goizueta didn't hesitate to turn to a "learning system" Doug Ivester utilized that we sometimes jokingly referred to as the "work penalty box." Once, Mr. Goizueta used it on me.

Leadership Insight

Capitalize on every opportunity to develop people—it's worth it.

On a trip to Vienna, Austria, for a week of review meetings, I received a call from Mr. Goizueta only hours after I arrived. He was upset about an incorrect figure he had noticed in an internal management report. Mr. Goizueta got straight to the point.

"This report is wrong," he said. "It needs to be fixed. Find out how this could have happened."

"I am already aware of the error, Roberto, and our financial people are working on the issue. As soon as I get back to Atlanta next week, I'll resolve it, and let you know the outcome."

There was a moment of silence. Then he said, "Jack, what flight will you be in on *tomorrow morning* to fix this problem?"

I thought that maybe he'd misunderstood. Perhaps we had a poor connection, or he didn't realize that I was in Austria. I said, "I have meetings scheduled here in Austria all this week—it's being worked on, and I will focus on it as soon as I return to Atlanta from Vienna next week."

There was another pause. Then he said very clearly, "No, Jack—I want you back here on the first plane tomorrow to deal with this."

Mr. Goizueta managed my mistake strategically, giving me very pointed feedback. He emphasized the importance of the numbers being absolutely correct when management saw them. He also created a consequence for me, albeit a painful one, in underscoring that my returning at once to correct that error was the top priority, and nothing else should take precedence. That served as an exclamation point that our underlying information systems had to maintain the accuracy and integrity to which we were accustomed. No excuses, no delays.

Mr. Goizueta chose to be incisive to make me find the source of the problem and report to him immediately on exactly what had transpired. He also put me into the "penalty box"—the discomfort of two long overseas flights back to back and a lost week of work in Vienna—for allowing the error to pass, even temporarily. Needless to say, next morning I was on the first plane back to the United States! When I arrived home, the first item on my agenda was correcting that error and seeing that it wouldn't happen again. After that experience, I paid much closer attention to reporting details.

Whenever I communicated about a mistake to Doug Ivester, as the words came out of my mouth, I felt him scrutinize every detail of my error. Doug would usually launch into a quiet lecture to remind me of a particular lesson about attention to detail or about something "not being done until it is done." After a while, I had the lessons pegged and numbered, and I'd think, "Oh no, here comes Lesson number 63." Sometimes I would wish that I could simply say, "Okay, okay, I know, Lesson 63," instead of hearing the whole lecture again. However, after hearing a lesson often enough, I focused on never making my mistake again and helping others avoid it too. It was the same with the dozens of other lessons I learned from other leaders. They taught me a lot about working to avoid mistakes, at least the predictable ones, and the importance, as a leader, of using the mistakes your people make as tools for enhancing and reinforcing learning.

CLOSING STATEMENT

Using these techniques, you will successfully retain and develop valuable people who will become strong performers for your organization. Developing people—and the excitement of building a team of exceptional, motivated contributors, watching them succeed and achieve great results for the organization—has been for me, and can become for you, the most enjoyable aspect of your leadership experience.

Developing people is hard and continuous work. If you manage it well, developing your people will become a straightforward and rewarding part of your leadership responsibility. Hold your organization's management accountable for helping to develop your people's skills. Don't let them off the hook! Your success, and your organization's bottom line, depends on it.

Brand Positioning
with Consumers

At the heart of creating value and long-term success for most organizations is the ability to design and develop a product or service to serve *a targeted group of end users*. For purposes of this discussion, we will call those end users "consumers." In most cases, consumers are people like you and me who buy items for our personal use. An end user also might be another company that buys your product or service for its own final use or to use in producing some other product to be on-sold.

A "brand" represents **a promise to consumers of what to expect from a product or service.** Brand positioning is *the process of establishing that promise in the minds of consumers.* Through effective brand positioning and related marketing actions, your product or service can become a recognized and valuable brand, known for delivering real benefits to consumers that are *distinct and different* from your competition. When brands *deliver* on their promise, they can create real power in the marketplace—and shareowner wealth.

Throughout my career at both Coca-Cola and Revlon, I saw how properly positioning and marketing brands can create value and build excitement in the marketplace.

The broad steps you need to take to position your organization's brand to build value are:

- Understand and specifically define what your brand will deliver to your target consumers. That is your *promise.*
- Define *exactly who* your target consumers are and understand their needs.
- Develop a brief, concise "positioning statement" that *personifies your brand and its promise* to your target consumer.

Only after you have accomplished these first three steps can you begin to drive your brand. Then you should:

- Identify and take the business and marketing actions necessary *to deliver on that promise* to your target consumers.

Here are the important techniques for positioning brands that are covered in this framework. They will include examples from my own experience and from other businesses that will help you establish, market, and build your own unique brands.

1. Define what your product or service uniquely delivers to your target consumers.

2. Define and focus your marketing on your target consumers.

3. Create a name and visual appearance for your brand that reinforces its positioning.

4. Build your brand at the point of purchase.

5. Build marketing relationships for your brand that resonate with your target consumers.

6. Prioritize and sequence the actions to reinforce your brand positioning

7. Avoid "positioning leakage" in marketing and advertising.

8. Build new layers into your brand.

9. Be aware of those chipping into the positioning of your brand.

10. Be disciplined with your marketing resources.

DEFINE WHAT YOUR PRODUCT OR SERVICE UNIQUELY DELIVERS TO YOUR TARGET CONSUMERS

Think hard about what each of your products or services *uniquely* delivers to your target consumers. Write it down in a paragraph or so. These key words and ideas will be at the center of *how you market your product or service.* Ultimately, they will become a focused corridor from which to build strong brands.

Consumers understand that the brand Coca-Cola, or Coca-Cola Classic, delivers three things: genuineness (which translated into "The Real Thing" advertising campaign), its ability to help make special times with friends and family even better, and great refreshment. These key points guide all marketing actions.

It's interesting to note that Coca-Cola's original brand positioning in the late 1800s indicated that Coke was a headache or brain tonic. The product was sold in the "drugstores" of those days and was positioned to relieve symptoms of a headache and provide an emotional lift. Point-of-sale material, signage, and billboards reinforced these benefits, and the Coca-Cola brand grew to be recognized.

What functions does your brand perform? How does it help its *ultimate consumers* function better? What exactly does your brand deliver—physically or emotionally—to those consumers? The sum total of your marketing actions (advertising, packaging, promotional materials, in-store merchandising, etc.) should answer these questions for your consumers.

As women grew tired of the fashion industry's unattainable ideal of beauty, Kellogg of Canada launched an unusual ad campaign in the fall of 1996 to promote their Special K® cereal. A series of advertisements attacked society's obsession with "thinness," while positively stressing fitness and health—including Special K as part of your diet—as the keys to a positive body image. This emphasis was very successful—so successful, in fact, that Kellogg's continues to use positive body image in the marketing campaigns for Special K cereal. Although fashions and diet trends have changed since 1996, the idea still resonates with today's health and fitness conscious consumers. It works because *it provides a solution for their target consumers' need or problem.*

Key Point

Strong marketing power is the result of taking the time to develop a clear and concise positioning for your brand.

Always think about your product as a potential solution for the consumer. Furthermore, always understand that this focus is entirely different from being centered on the internal attributes of your product, such as its technical makeup or how it is manufactured. Those factors may be foremost in *your* mind about your product, but they are important to consumers *only if they are translated into a solution that they value, and are willing to pay to have.* Consider that manufacturers such as Nike no longer appear to be selling just shoes and apparel to women; they are also selling *the image of empowerment through personal strength,* which is a "consumer solution"—offering women the chance to gain the ability to defy entrenched stereotypes.

When I came to Revlon in early 2002, we conducted consumer research to understand the current positioning of the Revlon brand in the minds of its consumers. Based on in-depth consumer interviews (done both on a one-on-one basis and in focus groups), we learned that the Revlon brand was indeed recognized and well known worldwide for its outstanding color cosmetic offerings, innovation, and excitement. It also was thought to be the "glamour brand" among mass-market color cosmetics.

However, based on our market research, we concluded that we needed to take additional actions to reinforce our positioning. To do that required articulating better what the positioning should be to attract today's cosmetics consumers. We ultimately chose to position the Revlon brand as the brand that will *create feelings of confident sexiness* in our target consumers.

This positioning of "confident sexiness" then became the *core centerpiece of all of our marketing efforts.* We based our print and television advertising around it. "Confident sexiness" would translate right through to our point-of-sale materials, our packaging, and *every touchpoint with the target Revlon consumer.* Once we were focused on the idea of confident sexiness, our marketing actions became more focused too. They became clearer, and more streamlined, and we were able to create a very positive impact for the brand with our consumers.

Leadership Insight

While success in business depends on action, *at the heart of exceptional marketing is* clear thinking, *particularly when you focus on how to position a brand.*

Your brand positioning must be clear and straightforward. You should be able to define for others what your brand represents in a simple statement. It must ring true to you and be stated in a way that consumers understand. Only then will your people have a *clear positioning* around which to build effective marketing programs that strengthen your brand in the eye of your target consumers. Unclear brand positioning leads to fuzzy direction for your marketers. That in turn results in a *scattered and very expensive* approach to the development of your marketing programs.

It is amazing what happens when you can describe what a brand means in just a few words (i.e., "confident sexiness" for Revlon, "exhilarating to drive" for BMW, or even the word "search," which to many users is the meaning of the Google brand) and when your organization rallies around that positioning to develop targeted brand and revenue-building programs. This saves time and money. It also avoids useless effort. To an organizational leader or general manager, it's a dream come true. An organization is then positioned to deliver on the brand's promise!

> **Key Point**
>
> *Throughout every one of your marketing programs, take care to reinforce exactly what your brand delivers to your consumers.*

If you are selling washing machines and your brand positioning is one of reliability, such as Maytag's brand, then your marketing should reinforce reliability as theirs consistently does. If your brand positioning is about the low cost of your product or service, then *say it!* If your brand is uplifting emotionally, then *show it!*

One way to define what your brand delivers to your consumers is to have a clear understanding of those consumers' habits as they relate to your product.

At Coca-Cola, for example, we took a hard look at the way our consumers moved through the course of their daily activities, how they spent their time from morning until night. We then identified the related "thirst occasions," an industry term for the moments during the day when consumers were most likely to want to consume a beverage. For example, a thirst occasion might mean wanting something to drink that provides a "pick me up" in the morning, like coffee, or it might mean needing to rehydrate after a workout in the late afternoon, or maybe seeking a final caffeine-free drink late at night. We mapped these thirst occasions, and then asked ourselves the question, "What products or packaging would be best suited to meet these various thirst occasions in the best possible way for consumers throughout their day?"

Formal market research is important. However, there is a tremendous amount to be gained simply by paying attention to how your consumers spend their time and thinking about their emotional needs. At Coca-Cola, we learned that our consumers spent a significant amount of time in their cars, driving to and from work and school and sports events.

We positioned our 20-ounce bottle, which was lightweight and, unlike aluminum cans, resealable, which made it a great "on the go" package to meet those thirst occasions that occurred when the consumer was driving. Coca-Cola was among the first to develop such a portable package that also could be consumed in more than one sitting. By understanding your target consumer's lifestyle, you can then develop products and packages that can be marketed directly to moments in a consumer's life.

Leadership Insight

Focusing on your consumers' lifestyles, their daily routines, and their emotional needs will help you shape what your product can deliver to them.

In the mid-1990s, The Coca-Cola Company had an opportunity to build and reinforce their Sprite brand in the United States. Coca-Cola decided to focus on the "clean, clear, and crisp" attributes of Sprite, the historical strengths of the brand with consumers that made Sprite an outstanding thirst quencher. By being focused on this clean, clear, and crisp positioning, our marketing team developed an advertising program that focused on the thirst benefits. The tag line of the campaign was "Image is nothing, thirst is everything." That reinforced the thirst-quenching power of Sprite, and at the same time poked fun at other products that focused only on their "image," rather than their ability to satisfy a thirst. That campaign was very successful, and it helped grow the Sprite brand at double-digit rates for the next three to five years, demonstrating the power of strong brand positioning.

At Revlon, once we landed on the positioning of confident sexiness for the Revlon cosmetics brand, we addressed the question of whether it was better to focus on the *emotional* benefits of our products or the *physical* benefits. At that time, we developed print advertising focused on the *emotional* benefits, a unique historical strength of the Revlon brand. We underscored this positioning in our advertising, portraying our spokesmodels to show that Revlon products would help a consumer feel her best.

At the bottom of our print advertising we also called out the *physical* benefits of Revlon lipstick and face makeup, the exceptional color, quality, and innovation that Revlon products offered. This balance of *both emotional and physical benefits* in the print campaign was an important part of our overall marketing strategy for the Revlon brand. This approach to communicating the total benefits of the brand improved significantly the imagery of our brands as measured by external research.

Key Questions to Consider

Have you defined what your brand delivers—physically and emotionally? What do you want your consumers to think your product *delivers* when they see your brand name or logo and your marketing communication?

Are you being persistent in telling your consumers what benefits your product or service offers them? Many times, I have found that marketers are bored by developing marketing messages that *explicitly tell* consumers what unique solutions your product delivers to them. As a result, they sometimes avoid taking actions to build the critical understanding of your brand. Do not let that happen, or your brand will never be as strong or well positioned as it could be. Exceptional marketing is not only about keeping your marketers excited and creative, **it is about building your brand in a way that creates specific memories about what your product or service delivers for your consumers,** in order to grow sales, profitability, and value.

DEFINE AND FOCUS YOUR MARKETING ON YOUR TARGET CONSUMERS

You must define your brand's *target consumers,* the group of people who will identify with and purchase your brand. Are they older or younger people? Are they male, female, or both? Are you targeting a particular demographic group or a group with special interests and needs? Once you have clearly defined the target consumer for your brand, build marketing activities that **speak to your target user in ways and through marketing tools** that you believe are specifically relevant to your target consumers and to their needs.

At Coca-Cola, teenagers are an important target consumer group. As you would expect, a large portion of advertising and promotional material is focused on teenagers. Coca-Cola helps this part of its consumer base know that the brand was designed to deliver genuineness and great refreshment *to them* and would help to make their time with their family and friends even more special. In the mid-1990s, we spoke directly to inner-city teens by creating "street teams" that showed up at local teen events in specially equipped vehicles with music and Coca-Cola products. Not surprisingly, these teenagers really liked what Coca-Cola brought to the party! This unusual form of street-level marketing really broke through the clutter of conventional marketing and drove consumption of the brand in many communities. Good consumer targeting and marketing programs that are relevant to the target consumer will drive growth.

Leadership Insight

Your competitors are probably thinking about your *consumers and their needs. You should do it* first *and* constantly!

Sometimes organizations try to change their target consumer demographic—and not always successfully. They try to appeal to a different group than the one they previously courted. For example, the General Motors Oldsmobile brand enjoyed excellent success with American consumers from the time that Eli Olds established it in 1897. Then in the 1990s, its appeal began to decline. By changing the brand's slogan to "It's not your father's Oldsmobile," the company tried to target younger drivers, but that target demographic did not buy into the new Oldsmobile marketing. In April 2004, the last Oldsmobile was produced. After more than a century, the Oldsmobile brand had been discontinued. It is important to be very thoughtful before trying to shift your target user base.

Key Point

Marketing resources usually are limited. Be clear about who your target consumers are and focus your limited resources on them.

As Revlon looked to strengthen further the positioning of our cosmetics brand we opted first to do some additional in-depth research. We wanted to know to whom our marketing should be targeted. We engaged the services of The Boston Consulting Group, a premier global consulting firm, also mentioned in Framework 2, to conduct consumer research. Rather than using traditional demographic profiling to target our messages, they explained that there were more meaningful ways of segmenting our consumers. Their research would be based on women's usage of our brands and our competitors' brands, and how they felt the different brands met their cosmetic needs—including their emotional needs.

We learned that the most important existing and potential consumers for Revlon brand cosmetics are what we called "trend-seekers." These women are the heavy users of cosmetics products, and they are not always loyal to a cosmetics brand or company—they prefer to experiment. Once we understood the importance of these particular target consumers, we set out to observe *everything* we could about that group of women, including how they spend their time and the different types of marketing media they watch and read. We also studied the target group to understand what marketing messages would attract their attention. The imagery in our television advertising became more stylish and current in its approach versus the more traditional image of glamour we had used before. We also made changes to our packaging to use sleeker, more modern designs and materials that we believed would better appeal to these women.

Key Questions to Consider

Have you clearly defined your target market? Don't spin your organization's wheels! Save time and money by knowing *how and where* the focus of your marketing should be directed.

Are you working to deliver your brand's promise to your loyal consumers? As you learn about the users of your products—both current ones and potential new users—you'll need to be thoughtful about where to focus your marketing resources. If you lose business from your existing consumers, you probably should focus your marketing first on shoring up your ability to meet their needs *in order to avoid losing more of them.* Once lost, loyalty is very expensive to regain.

CREATE A NAME AND VISUAL APPEARANCE FOR YOUR BRAND THAT REINFORCES ITS POSITIONING

Your "trademark" is whatever you decide to use—whether a name, phrase, symbol, design, or graphic—to identify and distinguish your brand from everyone else's. To ensure exclusive use of the trademark you select, you can and should register it with the Patent and Trademark

Office. The symbol for trademark is the superscript block letters ™ following the trademark name or graphic. You can use the trademark symbol ™ to notify others of your intent to register it during the registration process. You can't use the ® (Registered Trademark) symbol until your registration of trademark has been completed and approved by the U.S. Patent and Trademark Office. Visit *www.uspto.gov* for complete information about registering trademarks.

The first step is to consider the idea or mental image that you want your brand to portray. Think about choosing colors, font styles, and visual recognition for your brand **that will reinforce your overall brand positioning.**

The late, legendary advertising executive Leo Burnett believed that visuals appeal to the "basic emotions and primitive instincts" of consumers. Advertising does its best work by impression, he argued in 1956. Burnett spent much of his career encouraging his staff to identify those *visual symbols* that leave consumers with a "brand picture engraved on their consciousness." With unique and universally recognized Spenserian script, Coca-Cola used lettering in a way that showed the brand's uniqueness and genuineness.

With his smile, his once plump (now more stylishly slender) tummy, his baker's hat and his scarf, Poppin' Fresh®, the Pillsbury Doughboy™, an endearing American icon created by Burnett, personifies the "fresh from the oven" image of Pillsbury Refrigerated Dough. The character Poppin' Fresh appeals to children, reinforcing the idea that baking cookies and breads can be a happy and unifying family event, consistent with Pillsbury's positioning of their easy-to-bake products.

Key Point

Your trademark visuals, graphics, and packaging choices should be carefully selected and designed to reinforce the overall positioning of your brand.

BUILD YOUR BRAND AT THE
POINT OF PURCHASE

An important element of your brand's image is what your consumers think about how they actually *purchase* your brand. For many brands, building upon that perception is an important way of *building brand health*. What creates the "call to action" for the consumer to select and reselect *your* brand at the point of purchase? It is also critical to pay attention to when and how your brand is portrayed and merchandised wherever consumers can purchase your brand, whether on the shelf in a retail store, on the Internet, or from other methods—like catalog or telephone sales—that your target consumers use to shop.

Dell Inc. does a terrific job of building positive consumer perception for its brand of personal computers. Dell—the largest seller of computers in the United States—focuses on "the ease of purchase." They make it simple to buy a computer online and select the exact components you want for your new Dell computer. They then price and package the product and deliver your new Dell computer in a matter of days. This concentration on you as an individual and on your easy-purchase experience work together to build positive consumer perceptions for Dell. That strengthens connection to the Dell brand.

These actions have increased Dell shareholder wealth and allowed the company to expand into other areas—like printers, projectors, gaming PCs, televisions, and many other home and personal office products. To ease and facilitate that expansion into additional product lines, the Round Rock, Texas-based company decided in 2003 to change its name from Dell Computer to Dell Inc.

Another example of building brands effectively at the point of purchase is Seattle-based Starbucks Company, who not only create an excellent product, but also work relentlessly to ensure a wonderful consumer purchase experience inside their Starbucks-branded coffee houses. When you buy a cup of prepared Starbucks coffee, you find yourself in a warm, friendly environment where you have an opportunity to choose your coffee and have it prepared exactly as you like it, and you can interact with the person who prepares your coffee. There's even a functional name for that person: a "barista."

Key Point

Focus on creating consumer benefits that relate to how a product is purchased; this can be a very effective and efficient form of marketing.

The establishment itself is designed to provide amenities that allow you a choice. You can either sit and enjoy your coffee in a comfortable setting or take it out with you. This interaction with the barista and the homey social climate that Starbucks offers has built a new layer into the Starbucks brand through focused actions to build a positive experience at point of purchase.

Another example is the Victoria's Secret brand, owned by Limited Brands of Columbus, Ohio. When a consumer walks into a Victoria's Secret store, they see at once that all the products are merchandised beautifully. Unencumbered by restrictive packaging, the consumer has the opportunity to see the colors and feel the texture of Victoria's Secret garments. It's a beautiful purchase experience, and that *positive sensory perception* has helped to build their brand significantly. In 2002, we worked hard to strengthen the Revlon brand at the point of purchase. We did so by installing the new merchandising fixtures that I mentioned earlier in approximately twenty thousand retail stores in North America. These new merchandising fixtures make it easier for a woman to see the color and quality of the Revlon cosmetic products. By virtue of the way the products are arranged on the shelves, a consumer can more easily find her preferred shade of lipstick, mascara, or another product.

This was a vast improvement over the previous Revlon merchandising fixtures. Because of their design, the products and packaging were much less visible (and visually appealing) to the consumer. We also built the brand with our target consumers by including more pictures of the products and information about what the product delivers to the purchaser. This makes it easier for women to understand which Revlon cosmetic product is just right for them.

Think about how you build your brand's image at the point of purchase, and link that idea to how your consumer uses your product. If you are merchandising suntan lotion at retail, your point-of-sale materials might show the product being applied on a warm, sunny day at the beach. This visual image will encourage both *purchase* and *use* of your product.

Key Question to Consider

If you are selling packaged consumer products, are you working with your retail partners to strengthen how your brand is presented to the consumer at the point of purchase? This strategy offers an outstanding opportunity to work with your retail customer to understand *their* marketing and merchandising strategies. Gaining this understanding could position your organization to help the retailer better execute its merchandising strategy, build in-store positioning and imagery for your brand, benefit both your business and theirs, and build a positive relationship with the retailer along the way.

BUILD MARKETING RELATIONSHIPS FOR YOUR BRAND THAT RESONATE WITH YOUR TARGET CONSUMERS

You can strengthen the image of your brand by connecting it with people, events, music, or other activities **that you have determined (perhaps through in-depth research) are important to your target consumers.**

One of the greatest examples of these kinds of relationships is Macy's. When you think of Macy's department stores, you more than likely associate that brand name with the annual Macy's Thanksgiving Day Parade in New York City.

The Macy's parade has become a beloved American holiday tradition since it began in the early 1920s. Then and now, the parade has an outstanding family fun atmosphere, reinforcing the idea that Macy's department stores are a fun place to shop with your family.

> **Key Point**
>
> *Every brand marketing relationship either builds on or detracts from your brand. Choose only relationships that are consistent with the positioning of your brand.*

In a more recent example, at Coca-Cola we decided to associate the company's Sprite brand with rap music because, as noted before, Sprite was a brand whose positioning was to satisfy thirst, not image or hype, and many young rap listeners associate rap music with self-expression and being real. As a result, we dramatically strengthened that brand with teenagers, its target audience.

While most organizations do not have the resources that Coca-Cola has to commit to marketing partnerships, there are ways to create meaningful brand associations on a much smaller scale. For example, a local car dealership interested in marketing its automobiles to parents might form a marketing relationship with a local youth baseball league—or a local association of car enthusiasts. A local bookstore might sponsor or form book clubs.

Be careful about how and with whom you decide to associate your brand. Before you connect your brand with a popular personality, sport, or any other type of visible property, make sure that your target consumers' perceptions of that entity are consistent with where you want your brand to be positioned. NASCAR (National Association for Stock Car Auto Racing) appears to emphasize the exciting competition between and among its "family" of drivers and team owners—a perfect fit for Coca-Cola to reinforce its place during good times with family and friends. Coca-Cola came up with NASCAR-related packaging, vending machines, and promotions. Advertisements were shown in cinema theaters. There were special sweepstakes and electronic and interactive race car "rides" positioned at NASCAR races. There is no question that this marketing relationship helped grow the Coca-Cola brand.

Professional wrestling, on the other hand, might not fit as well with a brand like Coca-Cola, but associating with pro wrestling seems to work well for brands tied to raw energy and excitement.

Leadership Insight

Often people in organizations will choose brand relationships based on their own personal interests. Make sure the relationships you choose focus solely on what builds and reinforces your brand.

At Coca-Cola, we went through a very time-consuming process of refocusing our marketing dollars into programs and associations that we believed best built our brands. This process saved money, resulted in stronger brands, and produced measurable results. However, the process was often painful, as we sometimes discontinued long-standing marketing relationships that had been the favorites of certain Coke employees. We ended a number of particularly costly sponsorships of entertainment awards events and sports programming, where the benefits to our brands did not seem worth the investment.

PRIORITIZE AND SEQUENCE THE ACTIONS TO REINFORCE YOUR BRAND POSITIONING

For a new brand, or when repositioning an established one, it's critical to prioritize the marketing actions that deserve full initial focus, based on your understanding of your brand, its consumers, and the range of available marketing actions. Then, once a brand has a clear and effective positioning in the minds of your consumers, your marketing plan can be broadened to include those additional tactics that further build upon and extend your brand's relationship with your target consumer.

As I mentioned earlier, when we first began restrengthening the Revlon brand, we were very deliberate in identifying our target consumers—trend-seekers. Once we found them, we developed a television advertising campaign (a broad-reaching, necessary element of marketing plans for most big beauty brands) that would appeal to this specific group. Then we decided to promote our products in association with movies and launched the program mentioned earlier with the James Bond movie *Die Another Day*. It was a perfect association: In the movie, Revlon spokesmodel Halle Berry perfectly embodies the confident sexiness of our brand in her starring role. Yet, during this period, Revlon was presented with many other proposals to develop marketing relationships for our brands, from associations with NASCAR to beauty-related events such as awards shows. We let these opportunities pass—only *after* we had first defined our brand and reached out to our target audience through more broad-reaching advertising and promotional programs did we feel comfortable taking on additional relationships to further reinforce our brand positioning.

Leadership Insight

Prioritizing where to commit limited resources, capability, and time—to achieve maximum results—is one of your most important roles as a leader.

AVOID "POSITIONING LEAKAGE" IN MARKETING AND ADVERTISING

When you don't indicate *exactly what elements of your brand positioning* are meant to be emphasized to your marketing or advertising personnel, "positioning leakage" can happen. This means that your ads and marketing campaigns will fail to show **those key elements or attributes of the brand that will lead to increased sales.** This can be an expensive lesson, and it gives advertising agencies room to make excuses.

Key Question to Consider

Who in your organization "owns" your brand and is responsible for briefing your advertising and marketing agencies? Find out and make sure the direction is clear, precise, and consistent with your *brand positioning* and the *specific ideas you want to reinforce.*

BUILD NEW LAYERS INTO YOUR BRAND

First and foremost, your marketing should reinforce your brand's existing core attributes with the most frequent consumers of the brand. However, you can also look for new reasons and new ways for your most frequent consumers to buy *even more* of your product. These appeals will continue to help reinforce your bond with your existing consumer base, thereby improving on the health of your brand. Ultimately, they will help you *attract new consumers.* Over time, you will be adding more and more "layers" to your brand, with each layer increasing the brand's health, strength, and value.

When we restaged the Almay brand at Revlon in early 2006, we added a new layer to it—now, shopping for Almay products is easier for our consumers. To achieve this, on our merchandising fixtures in stores, we arrayed the various cosmetic and skin care products that make up the Almay brand by eye color and skin type; this makes it very easy for the consumer to find the right eye makeup and skin care products for her complexion. This new approach has helped to strengthen growth for the Almay brand by adding a new, relevant layer to the brand's positioning.

Leadership Insight

There is enormous value in long-living, enduring brands. Sometimes your organization will need to be nudged to focus on sustaining and building an established brand when there might be more excitement, but less value, in marketing a new brand.

It has been well over a century since Carl Conrad registered Budweiser® as a trademark brand of Anheuser Busch, thus making it one of the most enduring brands in America. It is a stronger brand today, nearly 130 years later, than it was back in the 1870s. The reason is clear; watch Budweiser's advertising. While they are constantly strengthening and adding layers to their brand, they first reinforce the brand's idea of *quality* by reminding consumers the beer is "beechwood aged." Then they extend their message with ads linked to *fun and enjoyment* (such as the funny talking frogs).

Key Questions to Consider

Are you finding new ways to reinforce your bond with your consumers? By offering new reasons to use your brand, you can extend the life of your brand and reinforce its place in the lives of your current consumers. This type of periodic "brand reinvention" can be a very efficient and profitable way to sustain an existing brand's life, consumer base, and profitability, as well as bring new consumers. It may be much less costly than simply introducing new products in order to increase revenues.

Are you allowing your expenditures to work twice? Virtually every expenditure your company makes *should be made to work twice*. Uniforms, vending machines, and delivery trucks can accomplish this. The uniforms of your sales or delivery force obviously must be functional and comfortable, but at the same time uniform design can reinforce your brand positioning through choices you make in color and placement of your logo. Vending machines for Coca-Cola not only dispense branded Coca-Cola products, they also carry marketing messages that reinforce the refreshment of the Coca-Cola brand. Delivery trucks carry the product but can also serve as moving billboards. Take actions to ensure that all of these types of necessary expenditures further your brand positioning.

BE AWARE OF THOSE CHIPPING INTO THE POSITIONING OF YOUR BRAND

No brand operates in a competitive vacuum. Your competitors are undoubtedly trying to eat into your brand's strength at every opportunity. Have you noticed how Fuji film built its brand with advertisements that highlight the fine resolution of pictures taken with Fuji film? Arguably, they captured this element of brand positioning from Kodak, their main competition. If your competitors try this, you should counteract their "chipping"" at your brand positioning by reinforcing those elements that are critical to your brand's success in a way that is *different* from your competitor.

At Coca-Cola, we watched the Pepsi brand with interest, as they often tried to chip into the positioning of Coca-Cola, particularly the Coke element of family and friends. In the early 1990s, Coca-Cola developed advertising that reinforced this aspect of the brand with a family of polar bears. Later, Pepsi tried to imitate this visual image by using bears in its advertisements. Arguably, in trying to creep closer to Coca-Cola's positioning, PepsiCo was stepping away from its own brand's core strength, which had always been youthfulness and excitement.

Key Question to Consider

Are you aware of your competitors and their brands' strengths? You may want to place more emphasis on certain aspects of *your* brand in order to decrease the value of a competitor's distinctive positioning.

BE DISCIPLINED WITH YOUR
MARKETING RESOURCES

Be mindful of how you allocate your marketing dollars. Helpful marketing analysis tools that allow you to predict results from potential marketing programs have been developed in the past several years. However, these tools, like most predictors, are not an exact science.

A more straightforward mechanism for allocating marketing resources is to ask marketing people to rank their proposed programs based on their reasonable best estimate of their likely impact on brand image, revenues and profits, and based on the ability of the organization to fully implement them.

Requesting a program ranking allows you to get a keen sense of your marketing staff's convictions about the programs' potential effectiveness. Consider using this approach to select those programs that offer the *highest potential payout* in terms of strengthening your brand's positioning with your target market and yielding increased sales and profits for that brand.

My experience is that marketers often build far too many tactics into their plans in an effort to use all available marketing tools. The reality is that your business can probably successfully execute only so many marketing programs at once because of the requirements placed on resources like your salesforce, distributors, required point-of-sale materials, and so forth. Therefore, prioritizing by ranking them in order of likely impact and then executing fewer of them more effectively will ensure better results for your organization.

Key Point

Prioritize your potential marketing programs and then focus on quality execution of the program(s) you've selected. This will maximize impact on the marketplace and the growth of your brands.

Your brand image, and how it relates to your consumers, is also important to your *customers*. Framework 5 focuses on building and maintaining relationships with "customers," meaning the organizations or companies—like retailers, wholesalers, or distributors—who buy your products in bulk and resell them, not end users. The framework teaches you how to sell your product or service effectively to these customers, and how to maximize your relationships with such buying organizations.

CLOSING STATEMENT

A brand's connection to consumers grows either stronger or weaker. **If you are not taking actions to strengthen your brand, then its strength is likely waning relative to your competitors.**

Your role is to develop, prioritize, and select those actions that will most *reinforce and strengthen* your brand to drive revenues and profits. Only by **having a clear picture of the positioning of your brand** will you be able to evaluate how a given program is likely to *reinforce* and strengthen your brand's positioning. With a clear picture of that positioning in mind, you'll also be able to help your people think more creatively about additional actions that will complement your marketing programs to strengthen your brands even more.

Creative marketing people will find lots of ways to spend your money. As a leader, you need to ask how their work strengthens the positioning of your brand and drives revenue. If an action does not reinforce at least *one important part* of your brand's positioning, don't spend the money or time on it. Recognize that *every* marketing expenditure is an opportunity to reinforce your brand. **Great marketing is not about style points or awards; it's about building unbreakable bonds with your consumers. It's about delivering on your brand's promise to them, through solid and creative marketing programs that link to the perceptions and behaviors you want from your consumers.**

Customer Relationship Management

Even with strong leadership and brands, your organization will not maximize its value unless you work to develop unbreakable bonds with your customers. "Customers" here means those who use your product in creating their product or who stock your merchandise and resell it to consumers. In this context, your "customers" might be manufacturers, wholesalers, service providers, retailers, or some (or all) of these.

This framework is based on the belief that every customer relationship is either building or waning in strength, just like the strength of a brand. Therefore, if your company is not strengthening its relationship with a customer, the relationship is weakening.

A key to unlocking value for your business is serving your customers well. The key to building strong brands and relationships with your customers starts with a relevant product or service; however, being able to *capture value* for that product or service depends on your

- people's ability to understand the needs of your customers;

- organization's ability to demonstrate to the customer that your product or service can add value for them; and

■ customers believing that your company deserves to share in that value, because it offers some advantage to them *relative to your competition.*

If your organization demonstrates these abilities, you may also gain opportunities to *broaden* the base of services that you provide to a customer and establish even stronger ties and mutual value for the long term.

For example, Coca-Cola's food-service (fountain) division has a very strong market position. The division sells syrups for Coca-Cola, Diet Coke, Sprite, and other beverage products to restaurants, sports arenas, and cafeterias.

In my experience, The Coca-Cola Company is unmatched in its ability to provide quality service that ensures fountain equipment is kept up and running. This service protects the quality of the product—its temperature, taste, the carbonation level—and helps to design equipment configurations to meet the specific needs of restaurants and other food-service customers.

The beverage services that Coca-Cola provides offer a very high profit margin for the restaurant. Over the years, Coca-Cola looked for ways to deepen relationships with existing customers, including providing access to consumer knowledge and research, and information about underlying trends and demographics that might affect a customer's business. One example of this might have been data on consumers' dramatically increasing interest in health and wellness, and that trend's likely impact on their choices in foods and beverages. This information could help shape a food-service customer's menu offerings. Often Coca-Cola set up visits to larger customers so that their functional staff could talk to Coca-Cola's leadership. At those meetings, we exchanged ideas on areas like financial planning, investor relations, and overall business strategy. Encouraging the face-to-face connections cemented the connection between Coca-Cola and its customers.

I recall one large customer that for many years sold Coca-Cola in its restaurants, but very few of our other products. Rather than offer

Sprite, they sold 7 Up, a competitive lemon-lime beverage that for many years outsold Sprite in the United States. For years, we focused on the basic service and delivery of the Coca-Cola products that they chose to sell, and then we worked to broaden our relationship by bringing to them ideas, market research, and expertise that helped them in other areas of their business. Finally, as a result of our outstanding day-to-day service and the valuable ideas and advice we offered, Coca-Cola was able to demonstrate that they would benefit from serving Sprite, a significant step forward for the brand. Later, as our relationship continued, the customer sold Coca-Cola's Minute Maid orange juice and our bottled water, too.

So by identifying and providing *basic underlying services,* and by constantly being on the lookout for ways to *deepen your connections* with a customer, you can broaden and develop your relationship with that customer in ways that could benefit both businesses. While your organization may not have Coca-Cola's resources and such a broad range of expertise to offer customers, it may well be that your organization's unique experiences and knowledge can add value to your customer relationships if you ask the right questions.

Something as simple as pointing your customer to a source of key industry financial information—such as an industry conference or trade publication—is an easy and inexpensive way to show your customers you care about their business. Learn their needs and capitalize on those opportunities whenever you can.

This framework is designed to help you build strong customer relationships from the ground up—as well as build upon your existing customer relationships—by understanding and honing the following customer relationship skills which require you to:

1. Understand your customer

2. Understand what your customer really wants to buy and why

3. Prioritize your customer base

4. Identify the people who influence decisions about your product or service

5. Listen for opportunities

6. Develop a selling strategy

7. Present your proposal to the customer

8. Develop plans and execute agreements

9. Schedule stewardship and review meetings

Building strong bonds with customers is hard and constant work, but it needn't be difficult or complicated.

UNDERSTAND YOUR CUSTOMER

I've heard estimates that more than 60 percent of customers who moved their business to a different supplier did so *because they were dissatisfied with the people who were servicing their business.* They felt that they weren't understood and did not receive good customer service.

I know from personal experience how frustrating it is to discover that those responsible for customer relationships have not been attentive to the needs of their customers. Employing people who have good customer relationship skills is not just a plus—it's a must.

Key Point

Constantly take steps to strengthen your relationships with your customers. If not, your customers will commit more of their energy and business to those suppliers who do.

One customer that Coca-Cola served was a wonderful and large chain of restaurants. These restaurants serve a varied menu of favorite American foods, including hamburgers and hot dogs. This particular customer had a long-standing relationship with Coca-Cola and was constantly interested in strengthening its own marketing and consumer relationships. Yet, I began to hear feedback from our sales organization that the customer was considering switching to one of our competitor's soft-drink products (apparently, our competitor was offering lower prices). Because this customer had always been loyal to Coca-Cola, I wondered if there might be deeper issues at hand—maybe we were not meeting the needs of the customer. I arranged to meet with them.

The visit was set up in one of the customer's restaurants. Over a hot dog and a chocolate shake, I talked with the owner about his business and its future. He pointed out that his business was under pressure from new restaurant competitors and his sales were suffering. The owner clearly needed support to grow his overall sales, not just sales of our products. Coca-Cola was focused too narrowly on the "product and service" aspect of our relationship with that customer. I realized that our relationship needed to expand to include other forms of marketing support.

Questioning him further, I decided that tapping into the marketing strength of The Coca-Cola Company might work for his needs by supporting their efforts to increase overall sales with exciting cooperative soft-drink marketing inside of his restaurants. In the ensuing years, we helped him develop better signage, more interesting marketing promotions, and advised him on other ways of creating excitement, including tie-ins between the restaurants and some of the sports and entertainment figures with whom Coca-Cola already had established promotional relationships. His business increased, and he appreciated our efforts and remained a loyal customer.

Leadership Insight

Asking questions and listening patiently and carefully—in order to understand your customer's business, where they want to take it, and how well you are serving it—is the foundation for great customer service.

The reality is that customers always look for (and expect) more from you because:

1. Every day competitors bombard your customers with options that may also meet their needs.
2. Many of your customers who on-sell your products to others are facing increasing demands for more service from *their* customers (or consumers).

In order to determine how your product or service can benefit your customer, you must have a complete understanding of that customer's business. Do your homework. Ask as many questions as you can and pay attention to the answers. Build your understanding by asking each of the following questions as a minimum:

1. What does success look like for your business?
2. What are your key business objectives and strategies?
3. How do you measure your organization's success?
4. What are the key challenges and barriers you face as an organization?

The answers to these questions will help you better understand the potential role your product and organization can play and **help to shape your strategy for how you sell your products or services to the customer.**

Working to understand our customers at Coca-Cola served us well with another large hamburger chain. Historically, it had been difficult to gain access to this company's senior management, which I believed made it difficult to build our relationship for the long term. We had a very capable salesperson on the account. On one of her visits, the customer indicated to her that they did not have well-developed capabilities to properly position their brands. We immediately saw this as an opportunity to connect with their senior management. We brought the customer comprehensive information from Coke's marketing department about how best to build and position brands in the marketplace.

As a result of that discussion, this customer, whose hamburgers were known for their high quality, recognized that their recent marketing had not emphasized the great taste and experience of their food. They were missing an opportunity to strengthen their brand by using marketing messages that highlighted the quality of their products and how they delight their consumers. After a discussion with Coca-Cola, the customer developed advertising and merchandising materials that conveyed their brand strengths, and the results were excellent. Moreover, because we had worked hard to gain an understanding of the broader business needs of this customer, we were able strengthen our business relationship with them.

Coca-Cola learned that another customer had decided to take their company public through a stock offering. We understood this process very well, and we offered to advise them about the steps involved in taking a company public, how best to position their company to the investment community, and some of the pitfalls of being a public company. Based on The Coca-Cola Company's depth of experience in public offerings, these critical insights would have been difficult for this customer to gain. As a demonstration of our interest in the continuing success of their business, we were able to *help them understand and solve a complex problem.* It cemented our relationship with that customer.

It is also very important to understand how each key person in a customer's organization might *personally win* by adopting your product or service. This means understanding more than just the direct benefits of your relationship to their organization; focus also on the *personal objectives* of the individuals involved. Such personal objectives might include creating outstanding results, career advancement, or simply wanting to "look good" in front of their boss. You can gain a real advantage by acting (within proper boundaries, of course) to help them "win" and in the process create benefits for their company and yours.

At one large grocery chain there was a senior buyer I'll call "Bob." He was very much interested in demonstrating to his boss that he had a real understanding of the demographics and shopping patterns of the chain's shoppers. It was obvious to me in my meetings with Bob that he believed showing this knowledge was key to advancement within his company. To help Bob gain and demonstrate that understanding—and in the process improve our business relationship with him and his company—we decided to share some consumer research and shopper data that would help Bob not only better market Coca-Cola products, but also promote other products in his grocery stores more effectively. This information included which items were best cross-merchandised with soft drinks to increase the size and value of the "shopping basket." At the same time, he was able to demonstrate to his boss that he had an increasing understanding of their shoppers. We created a personal win for Bob simply by arming him with a better understanding of his consumers. In the process, we significantly strengthened our relationship with that customer.

Leadership Insight

Your customer typically has two ways to "win"—professionally and personally. Listening for both will create opportunities to serve your customer more effectively.

UNDERSTAND WHAT YOUR CUSTOMER REALLY WANTS TO BUY AND WHY

Good customer relationship management starts with a clear understanding of the potential *solutions* or *benefits* your product or service offers. Therefore, you must be clear on how your product performs and builds value for the customer and express that in *terms that are important to them.*

One Coca-Cola customer's president was a very bright and capable businessperson who had spent his entire professional career in the family enterprise. He was interested in broadening his overall business perspective. While I was at Coca-Cola, he would often come to us for insights into our planning process, how we approached the development of information systems, and how we thought about marketing strategy. As a customer, he defined Coca-Cola's products and services more broadly to include support on effectively leading his business.

Realizing an opportunity to help him and meet the needs of our customer, we answered his questions and encouraged him to reach out to key people at Coca-Cola for more advice. Over the years, that interaction broadened the perspectives of this executive, and I believe it contributed to strengthening his business capabilities. Those capabilities helped him as he expanded the family business which gave us the opportunity to offer many more products and services to his company. It was a "personal win" for him, and a business win for his company and ours.

On the flip side, sometimes you'll find your customer's desires do not match up with your company's desire—or ability—to meet them. I learned this in discussions and negotiations with a large restaurant chain that we were trying to convince to switch from a competitor's products to Coke. We did a good job, I thought, in demonstrating the value of our products and services, but after a significant investment of time and energy, this potential customer seemed more interested in how his executives would be entertained in the future than how his business would be served by the switch. While we were very disappointed, we recognized that we were not in the best position to meet those needs. Ultimately, we were not able to convert this potential customer to Coca-Cola.

I believe that it is always important to focus on your core strengths and what you are uniquely able to bring to a potential customer, and not attempt to deliver services that you are in no position to offer.

PRIORITIZE YOUR CUSTOMER BASE

Your organization must prioritize your sales force's time. Be thoughtful about which potential customers you choose to focus on **based on the opportunity and anticipated returns versus the invest-**

ment that is required. Be sure that your people are cognizant of the boundaries of what your organization can and should do, and what incentives or solutions you can provide in order to gain that customer in a sensible way.

> ## Leadership Insight
> *As a leader, part of your responsibility is to ensure that your organization is prioritizing where and how its resources are invested with customers.*

While it is important to prioritize your customers, sometimes *size* is not the most important criterion. Little things can bring your company big returns.

When I became president of Coca-Cola in North America, I identified a relatively small customer located in the Northeast who played a very influential role in the trade association to which many retail grocery customers of The Coca-Cola Company belonged. Once I learned that this customer was an important "broadcast tower" in that trade association—other customers valued his business perspectives and opinions—I spent a particularly significant amount of time learning about and serving this business. Over time, we built a strong relationship, and this customer became an important and positive "opinion shaper" about The Coca-Cola Company. Prioritize your customer base in ways that make sense for your organization; it is critical to maximizing your impact on the marketplace.

Key Question to Consider

Do you have a good understanding of the economics involved in serving a potential or current customer? Your economics count! If you don't have enough financial resources to reinvest in your own business, your ability to meet your commitments to your customer or provide solutions to their problems will, of course, be limited. Be candid when you are unable to give economic incentives or concessions that the customer is demanding in order to do business with you. Be prepared to give up that business, rather than compromise your standards of quality and your continuing success as a business. On more than one occasion, I have had to look a customer in the eye and say, "I'm sorry, but we will not be able to continue to serve your business if it means reducing our prices and revenues so much that we could not continue to invest in and offer high-quality service to you and our other customers—the high quality to which we, as a company, are committed."

At one point in my career at Coca-Cola, we were involved in the renegotiation of our fountain contract with an important food-service customer. During the negotiations, we spent a lot of time demonstrating that Coca-Cola products and service were better than those of our competitors. However, in the course of the discussion, the customer focused only on the price of Coca-Cola syrup. It soon became apparent to me that our traditional approach was not being effective. We were just not able to get the customer to consider or acknowledge that the high quality of our service, our brands, and our overall support were worth a premium.

We went back and forth all day. I finally recognized that it was time to take a more radical approach to the negotiation. Late in the evening, I said, "If you are not prepared to acknowledge the value of Coca-Cola products and service—and there is indeed value in our offering that goes beyond that of a basic commodity—then I am prepared to resign the account, today, on behalf of The Coca-Cola Company." I gave every indication that my team would pack up their briefcases and return to Atlanta.

The customer was taken aback. The other members of my team tried not to show their surprise and concern, but I had tremendous conviction that the customer needed to be sent a clear message about our belief in the value to his company of our products and services, as well as the high quality of our people. The customer backtracked. He acknowledged that there was real value to his business from our products and services. Once he did so, we could begin to have a *meaningful* discussion on how Coca-Cola products and services could serve the customer in a way that would make economic sense for both the customer and The Coca-Cola Company.

This customer remains a valued and high-priority customer of The Coca-Cola Company. Their business deserves and receives significant resources. Nevertheless, our negotiations with them gave me important (and certainly tense) lessons about 1) having conviction about what you sell, and 2) protecting for your company the economics of your customer relationships, even with your priority customers.

IDENTIFY THE PEOPLE WHO INFLUENCE DECISIONS ABOUT YOUR PRODUCT OR SERVICE

An important part of the customer management process is to identify the people inside the customer's organization who impact decisions about your product or service. In their outstanding book, *The New Strategic Selling,* Robert B. Miller and Stephen E. Heiman (with Tad Tuleja) outline a proven sales system that is perhaps the gold-standard approach to effective selling. In this book, the people who impact decisions about your product or service are called "buying influencers" and they play different—but key—roles in the process. The following descriptions use Miller and Heiman's terminology for the four "buying influencer types," but the ensuing discussions of their roles as I see them are based on my own experiences.

■ **The Economic Buyer**—The economic buyer is the key person who can ultimately say "yes" to your product or service and not be overridden by anyone else in the customer's organization. Often the ultimate decision maker is the chief executive officer, but sometimes it can be someone unexpected, like an influential board member. *You will not be successful unless you understand precisely* who *will make the ultimate decision about what you want a customer to buy from you.*

I learned this hard lesson when calling on grocery customers for Coca-Cola. Often we would focus disproportionate energy on the chief executive of the grocery organizations. Yet, we realized after too long that as grocery companies became larger, more and more decisions were actually being made at the *division* or *regional level* of these grocery chains. By not calling on these regional or division offices often enough, we were missing key selling opportunities and often found ourselves "out of position" when trying to close an important sale. Finally learning about and understanding the shifts in the decision-making process in that customer's business led us to adjust our selling strategies accordingly.

■ **The User Buyer**—If you are selling manufacturing equipment, for example, the *user buyer* may be the person who runs the plant location that will actually use your equipment. People who are acting as "user buyers" usually have strong influence with the ultimate decision maker about purchasing your product.

■ **The Technical Buyer**—The technical buyer often plays an important purchasing role. This individual might not be the ultimate decision maker, but he or she will likely measure or compare your product against certain specifications. Often, the technical buyer is the key because he or she *makes a recommendation* about what to purchase to both the user of your product and to the economic buyer, the ultimate decision maker.

■ **The Coach**—The coach is "your" person inside the buying organization, someone who likes your product and can provide counsel on how best to sell your product to his or her organization. If you can, find and cultivate a relationship with a coach who has a genuine interest in seeing your product become successful; that coach can be very important in helping you make the sale to the ultimate decision maker in the target company.

I learned the importance of having a good coach when dealing with a food-service customer based in the Northeast. The CEO of this food-service company was particularly challenging. He was demanding on price and gave us little information about how to serve his company's beverage needs beyond his pricing requirements. We identified a person in the organization as a possible coach, someone who had worked with Coca-Cola for a long time. He understood that to get the best total service package for his company, he had to be willing to share the needs of his company more openly than his boss. He gave us insight that positioned us to develop an effective approach to discuss with his CEO. Fortunately for us, this coach had enjoyed a good experience with Coca-Cola, and he wanted us to grow our business with his company. That's not to say he wasn't out to get the best for his company. There was no question that he was, but he also understood that Coca-Cola had the knowledge, resources, and service capabilities to serve his business properly.

LISTEN FOR OPPORTUNITIES

The development of a selling strategy, or *how you will approach the sale,* starts with *listening.* Finding opportunities for your product to represent a solution for customers requires close attention to the customers' strategies, goals, objectives, and challenges. Be attuned to their responses. Ask follow-up questions to gain specific details. Listening attentively requires skill and patience, to avoid jumping ahead to your next response or your next question.

As you better understand your customer, you can better design your plan. When selling the benefits of Coca-Cola to a restaurant customer, we understood the time pressures facing restaurant personnel during their busiest hours. We also knew that the customer earns high profits on the sales of beverages. Therefore, beverage dispensing equipment breakdowns are costly. Coca-Cola's dispensing equipment avoids this potential problem by being designed for maximum "up time" and to require relatively little maintenance. As a result, restaurant personnel can be assured of a continuous supply of Coca-Cola, and they know that they will not lose high-margin sales during peak selling periods.

It's amazing how you can often translate discussions with a customer directly into sales opportunities. By asking the right questions of one large customer, we learned they were trying to find a way to take better advantage of the *capacity* of their restaurant sites over the course of 24 hours. The company owned its restaurant real estate and had no shortage of employees. We suggested that the customer create a special late-night menu that could be offered at their drive-through windows. Then we suggested a "package" by bundling Coca-Cola products with their easy-to-serve products. The program successfully increased their business and ours. Once you understand what your customer is trying to achieve, examine ways to tailor your product to be part of the *solution* to the customer's challenge.

Key Question to Consider

If your customers are retailers, are you visiting their locations and outlets? The more time you spend in the customer's environment, the better you will understand their business, which will provide you more ways to offer *value* to them.

One of my bosses at Coca-Cola, Doug Ivester, was walking around a small grocery retailer in the South. He asked the retailer what was his biggest challenge. This is a useful question that often reveals an immediate opportunity to provide a solution to a customer. In this instance, the customer told Doug that the metal in his produce display cabinets was rusting because they were washed at the end of each day. The cabinets were expensive to replace. Doug thought for a moment and said, "What if you were able to add a filter to your water supply, one that pulls the minerals out of the water that might be causing the rust on your cabinetry?" The retailer loved the idea, and, for a few dollars, he installed the filters. By working to understand his needs, Doug saved the customer a lot of money and cemented our relationship.

DEVELOP A SELLING STRATEGY

Building a strong relationship with current and potential customers requires that you develop a clear *destination* for that customer relationship. Your destination might be to become the top-rated supplier to a particular customer, or you may attempt to double your business with a customer within a certain time frame. Know where you want these relationships to lead and develop a customer business plan to get there. Ideally, this plan can be jointly developed with the customer. Then develop a *selling strategy* for how you are going to persuade the customer to work together to execute the plan

> **Key Point**
>
> *Develop a solid selling strategy which supports your destination and plan for your customer.*

Your selling strategy should always address the following questions:

1. What are the key benefits to the customer of what you are selling?
2. How does this match the needs of the customer and what the customer wants to buy?
3. What are the key selling actions that will move your relationship and business with the customer toward its destination, (i.e., meetings, presentations, events, phone contacts, etc.)?
4. Who have you identified as the customer's buying influencers, and who should be involved in the selling process?
5. Who in your organization can best influence these people and should participate?
6. What are the time frames for key actions?

Many years ago at Coca-Cola, a large customer decided to offer only a competitor's products in their stores. At the time, their decision seemed to be purely short term and financially driven.

The key to regaining that customer was the **clear and focused selling strategy developed by one of our best sales executives.** The heart of his strategy was to demonstrate that Coca-Cola was committed to the ongoing success of this customer even though we had lost their business. This sales leader demonstrated our commitment by routinely visiting the customer's headquarters to discuss the state of their company and to bring ideas and solutions that could help them improve their business. The Coca-Cola sales leader kept up this meeting routine over the course of at least two years. Finally, the customer decided to offer Coca-Cola products in their stores again. Through consistent and routine attention, we demonstrated that we were *always* interested in our customer's business, in good times and bad. Furthermore, by having an ongoing dialogue with the retailer, when an opportunity arose to regain our business, our sales leader recognized it and responded.

Key Question to Consider

Are you focusing on any potential barriers that may exist to positioning and selling your product to the customer successfully? These barriers can include any existing concerns or perceptions that a key person within the customer's organization has about your product or service. Another barrier might be a customer's existing relationships with your competitors.

PRESENT YOUR PROPOSAL TO THE CUSTOMER

An important element of your strategy for selling to your customer is the presentation of your proposal.

Framework 7: Influencing People, outlines an approach for effective communication. The steps include:

1. Make a person-to-person connection with your audience.
2. Build a broad context to serve as the background for your idea and to frame its importance.
3. Describe your idea or product, the opportunities it will create, and the problems it will solve based upon your understanding of your audience
4. Reconnect your idea to the broader context you outlined.
5. Reconnect on a personal level to your audience.

This model has been effective for me in developing my presentations and proposals to customers.

Leadership Insight

Customers want to be sold to, *and like everyone else, they want to be valued. Making a personal connection to your customers is critical to understanding their needs.*

A good example of building a connection with your audience occurred many years ago, when Coca-Cola invited NASCAR executives to its Atlanta headquarters to present a proposal for a marketing partnership. Rather than making the presentation in a conventional conference room environment, Coca-Cola's creative team, led by Steve Koonin, decided to make the pitch in an underground parking garage located three levels below the main building. For that occasion, the garage was converted to look like a NASCAR racetrack pit area, and seating for the audience was staged to make them feel they were right in the middle of a real racing environment. The NASCAR people understood Coca-Cola's enthusiasm for their sport and their business. I believe the unconventional setting for the proposal was a key factor in convincing NASCAR to become a Coca-Cola marketing partner.

Working to create a meaningful connection with the customer can show that you understand their company and what the benefit of a partnership will provide them. Even a simple, inexpensive visual can create positive emotion from the moment a customer sees it. A friend of mine was vice president of business development at Collette Vacations, a large travel company. He was invited to present a proposal at a small meeting of executives at the Smithsonian Institute for their travel program, Smithsonian Journeys. His company was considered a well-known, reliable, and "mass-market" travel brand; Smithsonian, of course, offered distinctive *educational* travel. So where was the opportunity for a partnership? Mike understood that Smithsonian considered his company "mass-market," a negative connotation to a luxury brand, so he designed the cover of his proposal to look like the cover of a future travel brochure. The design clearly showcased his company's understanding of the elite Smithsonian Journeys brand and the emotion they meant to evoke. He also incorporated his brand on the brochure cover in a way that did not threaten Smithsonian's brand. Mike was determined to demonstrate visually that the idea of a true partnership means creating value for *both* brands. Mike made sure to address the objections he knew existed to the partnership in the first paragraph in his proposal. He showed that Collette's long-standing brand value and its customer awareness were assets, not liabilities, for Smithsonian Journeys. At the end of the presentation, one Smithsonian executive exclaimed, "Why haven't we met with him and his company before?" The partnership still thrives today.

While Coca-Cola was able to use its many resources in the NASCAR example, Mike expended only the cost of the brochure and a PowerPoint presentation. Both examples show clearly that creativity, enthusiasm, and a thorough understanding of the customer's business fuels successful sales and marketing partnerships.

Key Questions to Consider

Are you considering the proper timing for your proposal? Does the date and time of your proposal work for the customer and *their* priorities? Be aware of the customer's business environment and any issues the customer might be dealing with around the time of your presentation.

Does your presentation focus on the customer's opportunities and problems—and not yours? Remember, the customer is the buyer! The focus of your communication should be the customer and how your product or service generates opportunities and solves their problems. It's about *their* needs—not yours!

Have you "presold" your proposal? An important part of the selling process is "informal" precommunication prior to the formal proposal presentation. Create opportunities in advance of a formal presentation to preview, perhaps informally, test, and gain commitment to your proposal with as many of the key people from the customer's organization as possible. By doing so, you might learn about potential barriers you will need to address, which can provide an important advantage for you.

Are you demonstrating passion for your product or service? Before your customer will be willing to believe in your product or service; they must be convinced that *you* believe in it.

Are there points that are so important to your organization that you must "fall on your sword" rather than relinquish ground? It is important for you and the customer to understand your limits. Making concessions inconsistent with the strategy or reputation of your company can limit your ability to support the needs of your customer properly.

Are you demonstrating that you understand your customers are people too? Knowing and understanding the key people in your customer's company is important. They also have strengths, weaknesses, and insecurities. See your customers as people with needs much like your own, rather than simply as a "title" or a just potential source of revenue for your company.

As you present your strategy for bringing solutions to the customer, are you making it their strategy? For the customer's decision makers to embrace your ideas, they must believe they have played a hand in crafting them. Work to communicate your strategy in a way that allows the customer to take ownership of the ideas and solutions you offer.

DEVELOP PLANS AND EXECUTE AGREEMENTS

More than once I have learned the importance of properly documenting agreements with customers.

In one case, Coca-Cola was slow to document an agreement with a customer; in fact, the agreement process was strung out over the course of a year. During that time, the customer's buyer, our contact at his company, was replaced by a new person. After a year had passed, Coca-Cola and its new customer contact could no longer remember or agree on the exact details of the agreement. This led to some very frustrating discussions with the customer, and though we ultimately continued our relationship, doing so required economic concessions.

This experience only served to reinforce the idea that you should get contracts of sale executed quickly and completely, so that you have a **clear basis on which to operate and move forward together** in your relationships with customers.

Leadership Insight

Execution is critical! Recognize that many people will have more energy and enthusiasm for making the sale than for finalizing the details of the agreement—or for overseeing its operational execution—with the customer.

Key Question to Consider

Are you completing contracts with your customers quickly?
The longer it takes you to document an agreement with your customer, the more time a competitor has to be disruptive and respond. Get contracts done quickly!

SCHEDULE STEWARDSHIP AND REVIEW MEETINGS

The purpose of scheduling and holding periodic stewardship and review sessions with a customer is to identify problems and potential opportunities, agree on follow-up actions, and to recommit your dedication to your customer. By encouraging feedback, the review sessions will allow you to evaluate the effectiveness of your product *through the eyes of your customer.* That should unearth any "loose bricks" in your relationship and uncover new opportunities to grow your business.

> **Key Point**
>
> *As a leader, stay up to date on your organization's relationships with key customers; feedback can represent threats—or opportunities—for you and your business.*

In my early days at Revlon, I had an opportunity to conduct stewardship meetings with our 25 largest customers. Our Revlon team and I met with one particularly large customer just after I was hired. The customer explained that Revlon was not providing service in a satisfactory fashion, and that we risked losing precious selling space in that important customer's stores. It was a very difficult meeting, but because we asked some important questions, we learned exactly what we needed to do to address the problems. In this meeting, the best way to learn how to improve our service was to ask, "Of the suppliers that serve you best, can you tell us what key elements of their service are most important to you?" Another important question we asked this customer was, "If you were standing in our shoes, from that vantage point, how would you approach fixing our relationship with you?" This question got the customer invested in *helping us solve the problem together.* In answering these questions, the customer gave us excellent direction that led to reorganizing and relocating our service team close to their home office, making changes in the packaging of our products, and focusing on our distribution and logistics capability, to serve the customer more efficiently.

Even tough stewardship and review meetings like the one I just described can lead to great outcomes when you ask the right questions and the customer feels comfortable being forthright. Eighteen months later, we had become a top-rated vendor with this customer.

Stewardship meetings are also an opportunity to ensure that the leadership of the customer's organization understands the value generated for them by your products and services. Create that understanding now, well ahead of your next contract renewal!

Be certain to ask the customer the following questions in stewardship meetings:

1. Is our product creating the results that you expected?
2. If not, why do you think that is so?
3. What problems are you encountering with our products or our services?
4. Has anything in your business strategy changed?
5. Do you see any other ways we can serve you better?

The answers to these questions may offer new opportunities to build your business with the customer.

Key Questions to Consider

Are you personally keeping in touch with your organization's key customers? A periodic phone call to important customers to obtain a quick status report on the quality of your service is very effective. Keep a handy phone list of customers you want to contact regularly. My own list at Coca-Cola consisted of 100 customers. It was part of my routine to call a certain number of customers each week to express my appreciation for their business, check for any problems, and ask about new opportunities for us to serve that customer better.

Can you create exclusive "currencies" for your customers in order to increase mutual value? Think of things that only *your organization* can do for your customers. Think of these services as "currencies" because they have value for your customer. For example, can you periodically bring the leaders of certain customers with similar interests and challenges together to share industry insights? Could you organize a philanthropic event that allows your organization to give something back to a cause especially relevant to customers' industry?

At Coca-Cola, we participated in our retailers' industry trade associations. The Food Marketing Institute (FMI) was an important industry association for our retail grocery customers. Many years ago, Coca-Cola partnered with FMI and formed the Coca-Cola Retail Research Council. This council was comprised of approximately 12 executives from various grocery retailers. With help from Coca-Cola, these executives stewarded research that would benefit the entire grocery industry. The research focused on issues such as how to minimize out-of-stocks—a perennial problem for retailers—and retaining store personnel, another ongoing retail challenge.

Sponsoring this forum with the FMI created a positive impact with the grocery industry for Coca-Cola. It enhanced our relationships with not only the 12 members of the council, but also with the industry in general. We established unique "currencies" for our customer relationships.

Smaller organizations might sponsor a recognized speaker on important small business matters to speak at a local meeting of community business owners—such as the Home Builders Association or the Chamber of Commerce—and invite their customers to attend as their guests. You might underwrite an award for the person in the customer's salesforce that increases the customer's sales the most during a special business anniversary month, or donate to a charity that your customer supports.

Are you always looking for additional ways to build new layers of strength into your customer relationships? Whenever you add a new service or bring additional value to a customer, you are effectively reinforcing the moat that protects your company from your competitors.

Key Point

Listen closely to learn about the little things you can do as an added service for your customer. They may be big for them!

Little things can count big with customers. Coca-Cola is a Super Bowl sponsor, and once we invited a customer and his wife to attend. (This was a normal and appropriate practice in customer relations for an important Coca-Cola-sponsored event.) On this occasion, the customer's wife couldn't go, and he somewhat hesitantly asked if it would be possible for him to bring his father (who was also involved with his business) as his guest. We said he could, and afterward, he told us that it was one of the great thrills of his life to attend the Super Bowl with his father. Of course, the Super Bowl doesn't seem like "a little thing," but caring about the customer as a person and doing thoughtful things that might be important to his or her life can go a long way. Recognizing your customers' family milestones, congratulating them on a business achievement, or providing professional advice or counsel to them or their family are just a few examples.

CLOSING STATEMENT

Through the techniques in this framework, assess whether you and your organization are strengthening your relationships with customers in a way that benefits them and unlocks value for your organization. Examine whether you are delivering to your customers *value* from your brands, products, and services. If not, take the steps necessary to build your organization's capability to manage its customer relationships in a positive way—one that serves and benefits your existing customers, and provides you with the ability to attract new customers.

Financial Strategy and Management

Businesses create revenue through products or services supported by strong marketing and customer relationships. In order to *maximize the value of a business,* revenues must be translated into **free cash flow** after taking into account all costs and necessary reinvestment in the business. This free cash flow can be used to repay debt or pay dividends to shareowners. **Effective financial strategy and management by company leaders is critical to ensuring that this happens.**

Leadership Insight

Leaders who understand that financial strategies and controls fuel company success will be best positioned to maximize their organization's long-term value.

As noted earlier, not long after I joined the financial division of the company in 1979, Coca-Cola leadership, under CEO Roberto Goizueta, made dramatic changes in the company's operating and marketing strategies. The goal was to strengthen the company's underlying performance and long-term value. This change process was initiated by taking steps to strengthen the company's bottling and distribution system around the world. We also took actions to strengthen the marketing of Coca-Cola's brands globally. We were very successful in making these changes, which took more than a decade.

We also knew that a fresh look at the company's financial strategies was in order. We made significant changes to the company's capital structure, dividend policies, and tax planning approach. At the same time, the company began a program to repurchase its own shares. These significant shifts in financial policies were accompanied by changes in the company's control and information reporting systems. These overall changes in financial strategies and management benefited the company's results during this period, adding several growth points to earnings per share.

By making these numerous and significant changes, The Coca-Cola Company was able to free up resources to support changes in the company's operating and marketing strategies.

As the benefits of the new marketing and operating strategies came to life, the impact on the company's overall results and long-term value was magnified even more dramatically. During this period, the company's market value rose from $3 billion to over $125 billion dollars, and the company was recognized as *Fortune* magazine's Most Admired Company. It was the effective combination of well-designed marketing and operational strategies supported by sound financial strategies that enabled that performance. This framework will give you a way of examining your organization's financial strategies and management. My focus is on **maximizing long-term free cash flow for the owners of your business.**

Obviously, the details of financial strategy, like other important functions of a business, can be complex and this framework will not attempt to address all those details. Rather, it is designed for the executive who does not have advanced training in finance and provides a way of thinking about, understanding, and asking questions regarding this critical area.

Effective financial strategy and management calls for leaders to:

1. Identify the primary goal of your organization
2. Know how to determine the value of a business
3. Develop a model that links the drivers of your business to how value is created for shareowners
4. Put in place financial policies that create value and are appropriate for your business
5. Encourage financial people to have an attitude of service, versus one of control
6. Encourage financial people to focus on the economics of the business and value creation
7. Communicate effectively with investors
8. Build effective control and information reporting systems
9. Recognize the importance of the many functional disciplines in your organization
10. Create compensation systems that link to shareowner value

By understanding these techniques, you will be in a better position to increase value for your shareowners. There also are two quick reference appendixes provided that amplify these ideas: Appendix A: Valuing a Business Using the Discounted Cash Flow Approach and Appendix B: Determining the Cost of Capital.

IDENTIFY THE PRIMARY GOAL OF YOUR ORGANIZATION

The main objective of any business operating for profit is to earn an attractive rate of return on investment for those who own the business. A business that can generate strong free cash flow on a long-term basis will likely see its value grow and be able to pay dividends to its owners.

> **Key Point**
> *The goal of creating value for those who own your business through growth in* free cash flow *is fundamental to strong financial strategy and management.*

During the 1970s, The Coca-Cola Company's stock price performance and overall business results lagged, especially compared to other periods of its long and successful history. In 1981, shortly after he assumed the position of CEO, Roberto Goizueta began actively and explicitly communicating that the *overall focus* of the Company would be *to create shareowner value,* as opposed to other more narrow measures used in the past, such as market share and earnings per share. This was a major shift from the past and required many managers inside the company to bear responsibility for the broader range of actions required to drive overall value for the company. I remember conversations among managers about whether the shift was a good idea for our long-standing, successful company. I remember that some argued we would lose focus on our brands and customers by emphasizing shareowner value.

However, Mr. Goizueta's focus on shareowner value had a dramatic impact on influencing people **to do all that was necessary and appropriate to grow the value of the business, including focusing strongly on our brands and customers.**

Under his leadership, we invested additional resources into the high-return international business of the company. We introduced new products like Diet Coke, and we began restructuring our bottling distribution system. All these new actions *created value.*

KNOW HOW TO DETERMINE THE VALUE OF A BUSINESS

In order to take actions that offer attractive returns and create value, it helps to understand, at least in broad terms, how to determine the value of a business. As any business owner knows, *cash creates value* because it can be used to pay dividends, pay off debt, or buy out shareowners or partners who wish to sell. **The value of a business today is equal to the expected total free cash flows of the business over its lifetime.**

While the process of determining the value of a business can be fairly complex, it is most important to understand that the value of the business is **equal to the total cash expected to be generated by the business over the long term,** after any required reinvestment in buildings, equipment, other fixed assets, and working capital (accounts receivable from customers, inventory, etc.).

Value is equal to the total of a business's projected "cash-ins," minus "cash-outs," for all years into the future—in other words, its anticipated free cash flow. For more detailed information on the process of determining the value of a business, please refer to Appendix A.

DEVELOP A MODEL THAT LINKS THE DRIVERS OF YOUR BUSINESS TO HOW VALUE IS CREATED FOR SHAREOWNERS

People inside your organization may not know intuitively how their actions can create value. Encourage them to learn by using a model to show them **how their actions link to creating shareowner value.**

Leadership Insight

As the leader, you must help make clear to your people the link between their actions and the creation of value for your company.

Coca-Cola's value-creation model was based on the principle that **maximizing the free cash flow generated over time by the business creates value.** We demonstrated that the "key drivers" that *generate* cash are:

- the sales volume of the product or service that you sell—in our case, Coca-Cola syrups and concentrates, (which is a function of industry growth and market share); and
- the pricing of your products and services;

  less:
  - the cost of goods sold;
  - selling, general, and administrative expenses; and
  - taxes.

At Coca-Cola, our model pointed out that the key drivers that *utilize* cash are:

- the amount of capital investment, including plant and equipment, required to sustain and grow the business;
- working capital requirements, including investment in accounts receivable and inventory;
- other ongoing investments, including investment in information systems; and
- the cost of any business acquisitions, including goodwill.

At Coca-Cola, we made dozens and dozens of presentations to demonstrate to both financial and operating personnel the importance of maximizing long-term free cash flow, and its resulting impact on the value of our company.

By having a model that shows what utilizes cash flow people will have a clearer understanding of what steps to take to minimize unnecessary investments. At Coca-Cola, our focus on free cash flow led to **dramatic reductions in inventory levels and other forms of working capital,** freeing up hundreds of millions of dollars in cash. These resources and our value creation model enabled and encouraged us to invest *more* in our very profitable brands and in high-return soft-drink sales equipment like vending machines. We also invested significantly more in acquiring bottlers of Coca-Cola. We later resold them, and in the process earned excellent financial returns. We undertook this process, however, primarily in order to place these bottlers in the hands of stronger ownership groups that would be more effective at growing Coca-Cola brands in their bottling territory. This strategy was critical in accelerating the overall growth of the company.

Key Question to Consider

Does your organization have a narrow-minded focus on earnings per share as the only key indicator of performance? A one-dimensional short-term focus on earnings per share often leads to underinvesting in high-return areas that create value. Focus attention on long-term free cash flow as a key driver of value. Take advantage of value-creating opportunities, such as taking steps to manage capital more efficiently. Invest more in high-return areas that support your strategy. In addition, beware of actions that have the effect of increasing reported "book" earnings while reducing value-creating cash flow.

Key Point

Long-term cash flow is king!

PUT IN PLACE FINANCIAL POLICIES THAT CREATE VALUE AND ARE APPROPRIATE FOR YOUR BUSINESS

In the early 1980s, as we worked to change Coca-Cola's financial strategies, we recognized that one critical element to be changed were our financial *policies,* which describe **how a company effectively and efficiently secures and protects the capital necessary to support and maximize the value of its business.**

Historically, The Coca-Cola Company had been relatively conservative in its financial policies. The company chose to employ relatively little debt on its balance sheet and paid out a very high percentage of earnings in the form of dividends to its shareowners. In the 1980s, however, we saw an opportunity to update our financial policies to support higher levels of reinvestment in our soft-drink business. We also saw an opportunity to create a more efficient capital structure, which would reduce the overall cost of the company's capital and increase the value of the company. In order to assess possible changes to our financial policies, we developed a financial model using the new—at the time—and exciting Lotus computer spreadsheet tools. Our financial model allowed us to set up and change important elements of the company's financial strategy on a computer screen and instantly see the impact of those changes in financial strategy on the company's key long-term financial measures—free cash flow, return on equity, earnings per share, and a projected value of the company's stock price.

By becoming adept at using this interactive tool, Doug Ivester, then a senior executive of the company, and I were able to walk our senior leadership through various changes to financial policies—changes that related to maximizing long-term cash flow and, therefore, the company's value.

We tested assumptions involving investing more money in high-return areas of the company, such as our international business, and we could immediately see the projected impact on our long-term financial results. We also tested the impact of changes in our capital structure, our dividend policy, and other important financial policy areas. By using this tool in communicating the anticipated benefits to our senior leadership, they were very supportive of these changes being made inside of our company. The changes made to the company's financial policies, along with changes to other financial and operational strategies, played an important role in accelerating the earnings-per-share growth rate of the company from its historical rate of approximately 10 percent to approximately 15 to 20 percent, and the changes significantly increased cash flow and shareowner value.

Understanding the different financial policies your organization can employ is critical. Following are keys areas of financial policy.

Create a Capital Structure That Maximizes Value for Your Shareowners

You can create significant value for your company by having a capital structure appropriate for your business that reduces your company's overall cost of capital, or funds.

There are two basic sources of capital for your business: 1) borrowed funds, or debt, and 2) equity capital provided by shareowners. Therefore, the most important decision when creating a capital structure for your business is the mix between debt and shareowner equity.

The cost of debt and equity capital depends upon the returns your lenders and shareowners expect in return. Borrowed funds cost less than equity capital because lenders, who get paid first, can be more certain of receiving their interest and principal payments. Shareowners rely on dividends, gains in the value of their stock, or the actual sale of their investment in the business, all of which are less certain. As a result, shareowners bear more risk—and typically expect a larger return—compared to lenders, who typically expect a lesser return.

Your company's overall cost of capital is the average of the cost of debt and the cost of equity capital, weighted by the proportion that each represents in your capital structure. You can reduce your company's overall cost of capital, and therefore increase the value of your business, by seeking out and using lower-cost debt in your company's capital structure. This only makes sense, of course, when you're in a position to meet the interest and principal obligations of your company safely.

Knowing your overall cost of capital is also important because this is the minimum **required rate of return** or "hurdle rate" you should require on investments of capital (e.g., investments in fixed assets) in your business. If capital investments in your business earn this minimum required rate of return, they will generate enough funds back to the company to help it satisfy its obligations to both lenders and shareowners. **Be disciplined about not committing resources to low-return capital projects and investments**—in other words, projects with projected rates of return below your company's overall cost of capital—unless there is some other compelling reason to do so.

For more detailed information on how to determine the cost of capital for your business, please refer to Appendix B.

In many large consumer products companies, debt represents 30 to 60 percent of their capital structure. Some industries and companies with very strong cash flow characteristics will utilize even higher levels of debt or financial leverage; industries and companies with greater business risk generally use less.

Key Point

Be disciplined about not committing resources to low-return capital projects and investments.

From 1981 to 1999, Coca-Cola went from virtually no debt in our capital structure to the point where debt represented 35 percent of total capital in 1999. As mentioned earlier, these borrowings significantly reduced our overall cost of capital from approximately 14 percent to 11 percent and provided the funds necessary to acquire Coca-Cola bottlers and resell them to stronger owners.

Minimize the cost of borrowed funds through efficient use of the debt markets, establishing good relationships with the lending community, and by timing your borrowings effectively.

Depending on the size and scope of your business and the expertise available to your organization, effective treasury management techniques can be very important to minimizing your company's cost of borrowed funds.

Maximize the Rate to Convert Foreign Currency Earnings into U.S. Dollars

For U.S.-based businesses with international operations, maximizing the rate at which you convert foreign currency earnings into dollars is very important to maximizing long-term cash flow. Businesses with predominately American shareowners that have operations based in non-U.S. currencies should consider practices that protect against the near-term impact of fluctuating currencies on the dollar value of assets and profit streams denominated in foreign currencies. In order to offset the economic impact on your company, you could choose to rely on higher inflation rates in non-U.S. locations causing local asset values to increase, which should, over the long term, tend to offset the effect of devaluing local currencies.

Similarly, local inflation may also allow you to realize price increases locally over the long term, thereby increasing local currency revenues and protecting the dollar value of your profit streams and, therefore, the value of your company.

In both circumstances, you are taking advantage of the natural hedging that results from the tendency of foreign exchange rates, when compared to the U.S. dollar, to move in line with the difference between local inflation rates and U.S. inflation rates.

Active approaches to protecting the dollar value of international assets and profit streams utilize financial tools such as non-U.S.-based borrowings; "puts," which act like insurance contracts covering the risk of currency devaluation; "calls," which give you the right to buy certain currencies at predetermined rates; and forward exchange contracts, which lock in pre-determined rates of exchange at points in time in the future. Those tools can help insulate your company from swings in currency movements. A competent treasury staff or your bankers can help you make these important judgments.

Tax Planning and Management

Tax planning and management is the process of analyzing and taking appropriate and legal steps to improve the overall economics of a business decision by minimizing federal, state, local, and other forms of taxes. This process is crucial to maximizing the after-tax free cash flow of a business—and therefore its value. However, this area of financial policy is often overlooked simply because many business decisions—such as where to geographically locate an operation, how to legally structure a new business entity, how to borrow funds, and many other day-to-day actions—have significant tax consequences of which general managers and nonfinancial people have not been made aware. Get advice from a tax expert in order to increase your own awareness of how your organization can maximize its value in this area.

Create a Dividend Policy That Matches Business Reinvestment Requirements

Once you have determined the appropriate capital structure for your business, maximize value by reinvesting in projects that are consistent with your strategy and are projected to earn rates of return above your overall cost of capital.

Excess funds—funds that you expect to be available after reinvestment requirements, interest, and principal payments—can be used to pay dividends to shareowners. The percentage of your earnings paid out in dividends is called the "dividend payout ratio." **Your payout**

ratio should be set at a level that allows for necessary reinvestment in your business.

Key Point

Setting your dividend payout ratio too high and underinvesting in your business reduces shareowner value. Paying out too little in dividends in order to invest in off-strategy or low-return projects also reduces value.

Historically, The Coca-Cola Company paid out 65 percent of earnings in the form of dividends. Essentially, we were underinvesting in our high-return business. Beginning in 1983, the company began gradually reducing the payout ratio to approximately 35 percent. By increasing the dividend at a slower rate than earnings, more funds were made available for investment in the high-return soft-drink business (including Coke machines, bottling equipment, and delivery trucks) and buying back company stock, which created significant value for shareowners.

This significant shift in financial strategy required careful communication with shareowners. As you would expect, they wanted reassurance that slowing the rate of dividend growth to invest more in our soft-drink business would be good for them. We illustrated that the return on capital invested in our business was well above 20 percent and, therefore, these investments, whether in Coca-Cola vending machines or new brands, would have a positive impact on the value of Coca-Cola stock over the long term. Undoubtedly, some investors sold their positions in Coca-Cola, preferring the certainty of higher dividends. However, most investors agreed with the assessment that the shift in financial strategy would create long-term value, and those that held our stock were rewarded with a significant long-term increase in the value of their Coca-Cola investment.

Consider the Repurchase of Your Company's Stock

As noted previously, there is an optimum capital structure for your company that utilizes debt in amounts appropriate for the risk of your business. When your company has excess cash or debt capacity beyond what is required for reinvestment in your business, you may wish to consider buying back your own stock. In these circumstances, using the excess financial resources of your company (excess cash or debt capacity) to buy back your stock may allow your company to maintain its *optimum capital structure* (the most appropriate balance of debt and equity capital for your business). Doing this can minimize your overall cost of capital and create value for your shareowners. Think about it this way: When you foresee excess cash or borrowing capacity, your company can create value by utilizing low-cost borrowings (realizing that interest costs are tax deductible) to buy your own stock. You would do this in order to earn a return on your own stock higher than your after-tax cost of borrowed funds. It should be noted here that there are likely to be other financial, accounting, and legal considerations that should factor into your consideration of stock repurchase.

At Coca-Cola, we bought back about one-third of the company's stock in open market purchases over the course of 15 years at an average price of $10–15 per share. At this writing, Coca-Cola stock trades above $45 per share, so it was an excellent investment by the company, significantly benefiting the remaining shareowners.

Manage Your Company's Investor Relations Program

Effective investor relations provide investors with a clear understanding of your company's performance and prospects for growth; this reduces potential uncertainty and "information risk" surrounding your stock. By reducing this risk, investors will implicitly reduce the risk premium and expected return they expect from your stock, increasing the value of your business.

> **Leadership Insight**
>
> *People will find lots of reasons for limiting communication with investors. Thoughtful and open communication will help achieve a fair valuation for your stock.*

During the late 1970s, the company did not communicate much to Wall Street. The company had been historically inclined towards privacy, and high raw material prices meant there was little good news to share. However, when Coca-Cola changed its business and financial strategies during the 1980s, the company decided to be proactive and step up its communication with the investment community. Coca-Cola provided expanded information on its operations around the world to give investors a much better understanding of how the company was approaching enhancing revenue growth and profitability. I believe this much more active approach to investor relations enhanced the company's valuation during the course of the next ten years. I discuss investor relations in more detail later in this framework.

Key Question to Consider

Are your company's financial policies and strategies standing in the way of creating value? Be aware of personal perceptions regarding debt and dividends that affect how the leadership of your organization views its financial policies.

VALUE CREATION MODEL (CHART)

The following chart summarizes the key elements of how value is created through maximizing cash generated, effectively managing the reinvestment required to support the business, and utilizing effective financial policies.

FIGURE 6.1 *Value Creation Model (Chart)*

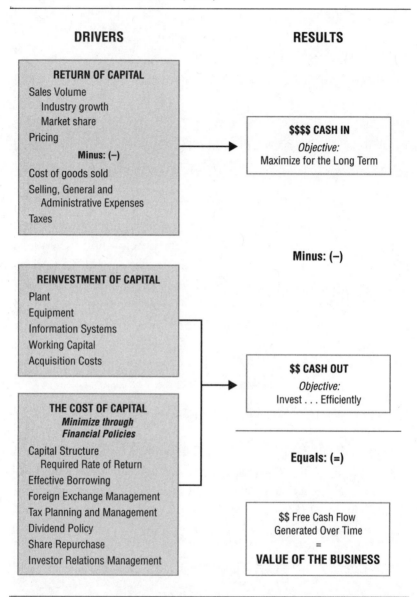

This Value Creation Model is based on work done by Stern Stewart & Co., a global consulting firm based in New York. Stern Stewart & Co. can be found at *www.sternstewart.com.*

ENCOURAGE FINANCIAL PEOPLE TO HAVE AN ATTITUDE OF SERVICE, VERSUS ONE OF CONTROL

Too often, financial people see their only role as implementing financial *controls* as opposed to also providing financial *services* to operating units. In other words, they cultivate a "control first" mentality. As a result, operating people often resist the involvement of financial people in "their corner" of the business.

On the other hand, when financial people provide meaningful services to operators as a matter of course—such as analysis of capital projects, costs, pricing, or competitive studies—they are more likely to be welcomed as members of the broader management team. As a result, financial people are then better positioned to provide necessary financial controls because they are *involved* in the business.

Leadership Insight

In order to add maximum value and *provide controls, the orientation of financial people should be on control through service, as opposed to service through* control.

At Coca-Cola, we set an objective for our financial people to be "invited to the table" of operating management. Beginning in 1981, we held a series of meetings with all of our financial managers, focusing on their skills in communication, project management, financial analysis, business valuation modeling, and negotiating—all specifically designed to support the operating side of the business. These skills ultimately helped the financial team contribute much more to the success of the business. One leadership seminar focused on their ability to help develop and coach the people who they managed. The meetings were very successful in building the next generation of financial people at Coca-Cola.

ENCOURAGE FINANCIAL PEOPLE TO FOCUS ON THE ECONOMICS OF THE BUSINESS AND VALUE CREATION

Your financial people should be thinking of actions to maximize long-term free cash flow—for example, reducing costs, eliminating excess investment in accounts receivable and inventories, ensuring the overall efficient use of capital, and providing analysis and recommendations related to pricing.

Financial people were important to the production strategy for The Coca-Cola Company by determining locations around the world that offered economic advantages for companies willing to relocate their manufacturing and production activities. After extensive analysis, Coca-Cola decided to centralize production of beverage syrups and concentrates into several international locations. The company gained production synergies and financial benefits thanks, in part, to financial people who understood the importance of maximizing the company's long-term cash flow. Ensure that the focus of your financial people is on the economics of your business and cash flow to maximize value.

COMMUNICATE EFFECTIVELY WITH INVESTORS

There are several guiding principles for a successful investor relations program.

1. **Recognize the nature of security analysts**—Analysts, whether at brokerage firms or investment management firms, are typically financial model-oriented, analytical, and sometimes very cynical by nature, given how often companies disappoint investors. At times, it was challenging to deal with certain analysts who followed Coca-Cola, but we found that providing a significant amount of facts and data gave substance to our view of the company's ability to generate strong financial results and encouraged a more accurate stock valuation.

Communicate your growth prospects using a value-creation model tailored to *your* business. It will give analysts a constructive way of thinking about, and valuing, your business. Treat all investor questions with respect—by doing so you will be more likely to get coverage that is fair and accurate.

2. **Involve your operating people in communication with investors**—To lend credibility to your presentations, draw upon your key people to expose security analysts and other investors to the nuts and bolts of your business. At Coca-Cola in 1983, we held an analyst meeting for approximately 200 investors. We decided to conduct the meeting at an unusual venue—a Coca-Cola bottling plant in Boston, Massachusetts. The leaders of the bottling operation made key presentations in a "conference room" that bottling company personnel built, its walls made of tens of thousands of cans of Coca-Cola. The meeting—and the discussion of our plans to grow our business—made a strong impression on the analysts and increased investor confidence in our company.

Be sure to thoroughly prepare personnel for the key questions they should likely expect from investors and agree in advance on appropriate answers. At Coca-Cola, preparation sessions, which usually lasted for a half day, were sometimes more difficult than the actual investor meetings, but they really paid off.

3. **Take advantage of different kinds of investor forums to tell your story**—Use large group meetings, small group meetings, one-on-one sessions, and broker-sponsored conferences to highlight your company's potential. The larger sessions can be an efficient way to communicate large amounts of data. Smaller sessions allow more time for questions and answers. Both can be important to creating a clear understanding of your company. At Coca-Cola, we not only had a large, detailed meeting every 18 months or so, usually held in Atlanta or New York City, but we also held smaller meetings with 20–30 investors about once

a month that included only short introductory comments by Coca-Cola management. Most of the time available in these meetings was dedicated to a question-and-answer period, which the investors appreciated.

4. **Communicate early and often**—When you have bad news, tell the story early. Ultimately, investors will find out anyway. Avoid credibility damage from telling the story late. At Coca-Cola, we always communicated significant disappointing news as early as possible. We usually got credit for being up front. As a result, we diminished the impact on our stock of the disappointing news.

5. **Be consistent in the amount of information you communicate**—Provide consistent amounts of information through good times and bad. Don't hold back during the bad times; you will lose credibility.

6. **Encourage investors to "invest" in understanding your business**—Provide as much information as you can about your business—without disclosing key competitive data— to allow investors to build their financial models. These models are used to value your company and your stock. When investors work hard to absorb the data that you provide them about your business, they gain increased familiarity and comfort with your company's story. This enhances the likelihood they will want to invest their capital. If following your company is too "easy," investors will skim the surface, hardly understanding why they should commit capital to your company for the long term.

Key Point

The more work investors put into productively studying and understanding your company, the less likely they will be to withdraw their support without solid reasons.

7. **Listen carefully to investors and their questions about the value of your company**—Ask them questions as well. Find out if they are buying and holding your stock. If not, try to understand why—it will help shape your communication with them. Also, ask investors what their "take-aways" are at the end of an investor meeting, their conclusions about your presentation. By asking these questions we would often uncover a misunderstanding about our strategy or our performance that we could correct *before they left the meeting.*

The better analysts understand your business, the less they will discount the value of your company due to information risk; generally this will lead to a higher valuation for your company.

BUILD EFFECTIVE CONTROL AND INFORMATION REPORTING SYSTEMS

Your control and information reporting systems should be viewed as *management tools,* rather than something that constrain your business.

Leadership Insight

The sum total of the elements comprising your control and information systems represents a management system.

A good control and information reporting system includes four important elements:

1. A planning and budgeting process that provides opportunities for discussion focusing on:
   a) where a general manager wants to take his or her business over a period of years (a destination);

b) key strategies or corridors of action to get there;

c) any foreseen barriers and potential solutions;

d) near-term actions that will bring the strategy to life;

e) required resources (e.g., people and capital); and

f) expected results

2. Decision-making corridors where levels of *authority* are matched with levels of *capability*, and where learning opportunities are developed through discussions about potential actions to be approved

3. Information reporting tools that measure results directly linked to your strategy, plans, and the "health" of your organization

4. Effective internal and external audit functions

A Planning and Budgeting Process

During our change process in the mid-1980s it became apparent that Coca-Cola could benefit from a *stronger planning system.* Until then, annual business plan presentations had been made by operating managers from around the world who often focused only on problems to be fixed. In my judgment, there was not enough focus on *the opportunities to grow the business* based on a clear analysis of current levels of consumption of soft drinks, consumer trends, the needs of our retail partners, and the needs of our bottling partners.

The company created a cross-functional team to develop a more structured planning approach and common framework focusing on 1) the economic environment; 2) underlying beverage consumption trends; and 3) what the key drivers of future soft drink growth in a given country, or market, might be. Then this model called for laying out a) the actions necessary to create and capture the growth; b) required resources; and c) projected longer term benefits. The approach led to much better discussion about opportunities to grow the business profitably.

Decision-Making Corridors Where Levels of *Authority* Match Levels of *Capability*

In many corporations, there is a "chart of authority" that spells out where in the organization resources can be committed. This chart of authority should be straightforward and simple so that people understand the limits of their authority to commit company resources.

Sometimes decision-making corridors need to be shrunk, as happened to me on one occasion I remember very well. As Coca-Cola CFO, I called chairman and CEO Roberto Goizueta at home one evening. I needed to gain his approval for an international currency transaction that we wanted to execute early the next morning. He approved it, but unfortunately, my timing for this transaction was wrong, and we lost money. Mr. Goizueta never said a thing about it until about a year later, when I again had to call him at home to discuss a similar transaction. Remembering our previous late-night phone discussion, Mr. Goizueta said, "Jack, you have proven to me that we don't do good business over the telephone. Why don't you come by my office tomorrow morning at eight o'clock to discuss this one in more detail?" He had shrunk, at least temporarily, my decision-making corridor by asking to hear more details about this transaction. As a leader, be thoughtful about the decision-making corridors you provide your people; match them with their current level of capability, and grow their skills through learning discussions about upcoming decisions.

Information Reporting Tools Linked to Strategy, Plans, and the Health of Your Organization

These tools include not only key financial and marketplace measures (for example, market share) but also measures of organizational health, such as product quality and customer and employee satisfaction.

One important management tool can be a "rolling estimate" process. At Coca-Cola every 30 days, operating management reforecasts the current monthly, quarterly, and full-year results for key business measures, compares such forecasted results against the original plan, and outlines any new planned actions. We developed and implemented this tool at the company in the early 1980s. Operating management resisted it at first. It meant a lot more work and analysis because it required a detailed reforecast of the business and financial results for each company business unit. After a short time, however, it became our most useful tool to manage the business. Create the management tools you need to run your business. Build them gradually so their implementation doesn't bog down your organization.

Effective Internal and External Audit Functions

An effective internal audit function is a critical part of your control systems. Internal auditors can help protect company assets by detecting actual breakdowns in controls; they should also focus on preventing such breakdowns by recommending the creation of additional control systems when necessary. Internal auditors can also represent an excellent source of talent for your organization due to the understanding they gain through working with your operations. At Coca-Cola, we hired dozens of internal auditors who ultimately became key financial leaders and general managers.

> **Key Point**
>
> *Explain the control systems of your organization as a* critical tool *for managing your business. You will set the proper tone for the management of your company.*

The management systems took approximately five years to build at Coca-Cola. While sometimes people resisted changing their routines and the extra oversight from our corporate headquarters, they came to be seen as critical to managing the business and maximizing shareowner value.

RECOGNIZE THE IMPORTANCE OF THE MANY FUNCTIONAL DISCIPLINES IN YOUR ORGANIZATION

As a general manager, financial manager, or leader of another division or department, part of your job is to translate operating actions into *real value* through understanding the basics of finance. Yet, it is also important that you understand the value of other functional disciplines as opposed to seeing them as constraints.

For example, when I was advised by my legal staff not to take an action, I always asked them to outline the legal risks and consequences on which they were focused that underpinned their counsel. The answers they provided shaped my thinking. By asking questions and encouraging quality interaction by building links between different departments through routine meetings, you can make your organization more effective, and thus add to its value. As a leader, you must set the tone for and encourage good cross-division communication—you will get to better answers and solutions, and your people will broaden their perspectives.

CREATE COMPENSATION SYSTEMS THAT LINK TO SHAREOWNER VALUE

Leaders must ensure that compensation systems **reward those financial measures that are linked to shareowner value,** such as free cash flow and rate of return on capital. Based on a model developed by Stern Stewart & Company, a New York-based consulting firm, "economic profit" is a measure that equals operating profits after taxes, minus a capital charge equal to your company's overall cost of capital, multiplied by the total capital invested in a particular business unit (see Appendix B). The *increase* in economic profit over time, or *Economic Value Added* ® (EVA®), is a measure shown to be directly tied to future free cash flows and to shareowner value. Because this measure tracks closely to shareowner value, it can prove beneficial to include it among performance measures used for compensation. As a compensation strategy, EVA can motivate the right actions to maximize the long-term and sustainable value of a company.

At Coca-Cola, in the 1980s, we created a long-term compensation system which rewarded executives based upon **EVA created over the course of a three-year period for their area of responsibility.** As a result, these leaders were motivated not only to take actions to grow profits, but also to be efficient in the use of capital because those who used the company's capital were "charged" for it. They were intent on earning a return on the capital they used that exceeded its cost. Once we had linked our compensation systems to measures like those, we told the investment community that our people had incentive to grow these important measures. As a result, the investment community took great confidence in knowing that we were focused on creating shareowner value. Coke was one of the first companies to adopt such a compensation system, and I believe it contributed to the sustainable value of the company.

CLOSING STATEMENT

You can create real value for the owners of your business **by building a financial strategy and management framework based on maximizing long-term free cash flow and then linking it to the operations of your business.** Effective financial management can create value even in advance of successfully implementing your operating strategies. As a result, you can buy time for operating actions to take hold. For each of the areas discussed above, I encourage you to seek financial expertise and ask questions to aid your decision making. Whenever some of these areas seem too complex, **bring the focus back to maximizing long-term free cash flow.**

Appendixes A and B should help you understand how to determine the value of a business and the cost of capital.

Influencing People

I have presented six frameworks for creating leadership success. The seventh is a linchpin for them all because success in any leadership role **will depend upon your ability to effectively influence people to take actions to achieve success.**

Your success will also depend upon your **ability to listen to and be influenced by others to take the actions that will benefit your organization.** In order to effectively lead, manage, develop people, market your brands, service your customers, and implement sound financial strategies you will need *effective influencing skills.* The truth is, you can't create organizational success alone.

> ### Key Point
> *Your ability to influence and to be influenced will be either an enabler or a barrier to your success as a leader.*

When I came to Revlon in 2002, the company had a number of key assets, including great brands and many committed and capable people. Unfortunately, there had been a significant amount of change and turnover at the company—some of it unproductive—that had led to declining revenues and profitability. The company was at a critical juncture, organizationally, financially, and with its consumers and retail customers. My first task at Revlon was to make sure I learned everything I could about the challenges at hand. Then I quickly began to communicate a message that would help keep people motivated and engaged.

The role of the new Revlon leadership team was critical at that point in the company's history. We needed to *influence the organization* and get them to understand and help shape a new strategic direction for the company and then take the actions we felt would begin to bring that strategy to reality.

We succeeded. Yet had we failed at influencing our people, we would have missed the chance to begin to improve the profitability of the company.

Leadership Insight

Immediately creating a picture of what success looks like—for the organization and the individual—positions leaders to influence others to move toward creating that success.

There are obviously many different types of communication that leaders use to influence people. I use a mix of them—such as one-on-one contact, being visible and accessible, large group presentations, small group meetings, talking to people in hallways and elevators, emails, phone calls, faxes, written letters, newsletters, and memos. Whatever communication tools you use, I believe that effective communication and influencing requires understanding that as people consider or evaluate ideas, proposals, and presentations, they will make their decisions based on two key factors: 1) the *merits* of proposals and ideas themselves, and 2) their very human need to be *valued* as individuals.

Thus, there are three broad components, or keys, to influencing people:

1. Understanding your audience
2. Organizing your content effectively
3. Building a connection between you and your audience

By focusing on these areas before, during, and after key communications, your impact as a leader will increase dramatically. After a while, you'll find yourself employing these practices naturally, and your preparation time will become less and less. First and foremost, you have to understand your target audience.

UNDERSTAND YOUR AUDIENCE

In order to effectively sell an idea or a product or persuade others to take action, you must work to fully understand why that idea, product, or decision is important or useful to them. Then use that knowledge and understanding to shape your communication.

> **Key Point**
> *Understanding your audience, organizationally and personally, is the key to effective communication.*

At Coca-Cola, we worked hard to understand our audiences, particularly our customers. In the late 1990s, one of our restaurant customers was positioning their company to make an offering of its common stock. We used all the tools recommended in previous frameworks to investigate and understand their business. We believed that as this customer presented itself to potential investors, they would benefit from highlighting their key supplier relationship with a strong company with well-known brands and marketing capabilities like Coca-Cola. The customer embraced our idea and later described the benefits of our relationship during their public offering, strengthening their presentation. By understanding our audience and their important needs, Coca-Cola created an advantage for them and enhanced our long-term relationship. Strive to develop this kind of understanding of audiences you are working to influence.

The following questions and discussions cover a broad span of ideas you'll need to explore in understanding your audience.

What Motivates Your Target Audience and Their Organization?

When I became president of Coca-Cola North America in 1994, our first objective was to grow consumption of Coca-Cola products in North America at a faster rate. This required strengthening the relationship between The Coca-Cola Company and Coca-Cola bottlers. Remember that the Atlanta-based Coca-Cola Company, which largely produces syrups and concentrates, is a distinct and separate corporation from each of the many companies worldwide that bottle and distribute Coca-Cola products. In certain cases, The Coca-Cola Company invests in these bottling companies, but usually that is not the case. As a result, the financial results and economic interests of The Coca-Cola Company and Coca-Cola bottlers are separate and different. Understanding the importance of what motivated each of us, we realized together through very in-depth conversations, that maximizing the *combined and mutual* long-term value of The Coca-Cola Company and independent bottlers—*not one at the expense of the other*—was key to both our interests. This understanding had not always been as clear before that point, and that was a barrier to accelerating growth. Maximizing long-term value of the Coca-Cola *system,* in a sustainable way, then became the common goal of both The Coca-Cola Company and bottlers. Once that concept was achieved, we were then able to develop strategies to maximize consumption of Coca-Cola products in a profitable way, for both of us. For example, we proposed to make intense investments in cold-drink equipment for Coca-Cola products, such as Coca-Cola vending machines. A well-situated Coca-Cola vending machine in a community would generate not only significant increases in visibility for Coca-Cola, and consumption of our beverages, it also was a very profitable undertaking for the combined Coca-Cola system. Key to our execution of strategies like this was the initial work and the many interactive conversations we had to help understand the motivations of The Coca-Cola Company, and also those of the Coca-Cola bottlers.

Key Point

Seek to understand the motivations of your important audiences, in order to create a platform for effective communication.

Do You Understand Their Financial Objectives?

When dealing with one Coca-Cola customer, it became apparent to us that a certain financial measure—productivity of their assets—was the key to their business strategies. We learned that the way they measured this indicator was by asset turnover (revenues divided by the total assets of the company). Once we understood that it was important for that customer to drive their revenues relative to their asset base, we were able to calculate from their inventories and annual revenues from selling Coca-Cola products that our products turned over *50 times per year* in their stores. In other words, each delivery of Coca-Cola inventory stayed in their stores for a very short period (only a week on average) before it was sold. We pointed this out to our customer and showed them that by positioning Coca-Cola to sell more in their stores, we would have a very positive impact on their overall measure of asset turnover. When this particular customer understood our impact on their key objectives, they committed extra resources to buying and selling more Coca-Cola products.

What Are Their Key Strategies and Challenges for Achieving Their Goals?

As the last example demonstrates, by *understanding* your audience's key strategies, you can *shape your presentation*. Tailor it to demonstrate specifically how your idea or product can reinforce those key strategies, and therefore help them achieve their goals.

How Might Your Audience Personally Win Through Your Idea?

By listening carefully to the senior leadership of one customer, we learned that having well-developed relationships with suppliers was an important part of their strategy. One particular executive viewed it as a personal "win" and a victory for his company to turn a relationship with a large supplier, such as Revlon, in a positive direction. We discussed with this executive ways to develop a more extensive relationship and grow sales of our products in their stores. We met with him to set up a "test bed"—a new marketing initiative in which Revlon products were marketed in different and more exciting ways. We then implemented what we learned from this test bed to reposition our relationship. Both businesses reaped significant benefits from this joint endeavor. In the process, this executive was able to demonstrate new models for rejuvenating relationships with suppliers—a personal win for him.

What Prior Assumptions (or Biases) Might Your Audience Have about Your Idea?

In my early days at Revlon, we scheduled a meeting with current and potential investors in New York City. Before the presentation, we did a tremendous amount of research to understand what assumptions the investment community had about Revlon. Our homework told us that investors had been disappointed by Revlon in the previous five or six years, and they felt that perhaps our management did not have a clear understanding of the underlying issues that had caused Revlon's performance to lag. So we spent a significant amount of our presentation explaining what we saw as the underlying issues that had burdened Revlon in the past. These issues largely related to breakdowns in the basic direction and execution of our marketing programs and not providing good service to our retail customers. We talked about how Revlon's new leadership team was very disciplined in its focus on the day-to-day details of business operations in order to ensure successful execution in the marketplace.

By learning in advance the assumptions and concerns about Revlon, we were able to address those concerns and show how we had the potential to create long-term value and provide good returns to investors from investing in Revlon common stock and our debt instruments. As a result, many investors chose to continue to invest their capital in our company at a critical time for us.

Key Questions to Consider

Are you aware of the perceptions of your audience? Those perceptions or preconceived notions are your audience's *reality!* Try to understand them so you'll have the opportunity to shape your communication to change those perceptions.

While I was at Revlon, we interviewed candidates for senior leadership positions. At the start of an interview, I would often ask questions to help me understand the candidate's existing perceptions of Revlon. Sometimes the interviewees would raise concerns about the credibility of the company and our perceived lack of financial resources. Once I understood their negative perceptions, I was able to demonstrate that we were building a capable leadership team and assured them that we would indeed have access to financial resources to generate growth for our business.

Addressing concerns and perceptions up front allows your audience to be more relaxed and feel comfortable that you understand their needs and will respond to them.

Are you arriving well before your presentations, talking to people who likely will be members of your audience, and asking questions that will help you understand their perceptions, goals, strategies, and challenges? Arriving at a presentation early can be a good opportunity to gain insight into the minds of your audience members. It's also helpful to get input from other people who understand your audience.

Are you staying late after presentations? This gives you a chance to debrief your audience—to obtain feedback that will tell you whether you were successful in communicating your message. This is an important part of understanding your audience and shaping subsequent communication. At Revlon, we held monthly operating reviews typically attended by 25 to 30 people. During these meetings, we reviewed every part of our North American business. After one operating review of a major new product initiative for the Almay brand, members of our leadership team informally asked other attendees for feedback. Several people at the meeting were concerned that the project involved developing and producing hundreds of new SKUs in one year, a very large number. Launching so many at once was operationally complex and required tremendous communication across all functions of the company. This was a valid concern. Revlon leaders then formed a new routine involving key people responsible for managing the project. They would hold a detailed weekly meeting and discuss every element of the Almay brand new product initiative. This small change, brought about by taking the time after meetings to listen for concerns, increased confidence in the initiative and enabled its successful execution.

Are you aware of who in your audience are the "broadcast towers"? Broadcast towers are people who *carry significant influence* with the remainder of your audience. These people can be either your biggest supporters or your biggest detractors. By knowing and understanding who they are in advance, you can choose how much time and energy to spend trying to influence them.

When I was president of Coca-Cola North America, I realized that a few small Coca-Cola bottlers carried disproportionate influence with the other 86 bottlers, most of which were much larger companies. I spent a lot of time working to understand—and address—the concerns of these smaller bottlers so that they could become a positive influence on the rest.

Do you recognize that people communicate in different ways? Different forms of communication motivate different people. To communicate well, you must understand those differences and use them to your advantage. Does an individual you are trying to influence require facts and data to relate to your idea, or is this someone with whom you need to discuss an issue on a more conceptual (or even emotional) level? When dealing one on one, try to be sensitive to how people prefer to be influenced. It will make you a more effective communicator with that person.

Initially, one of my direct reports and I had a difficult time communicating. Finally, I appealed to a communications consultant to evaluate our problem. After some observation, the consultant pointed out that this individual preferred a lot of facts and data—information was the key to opening a line of communication with this individual. Then, I was able to change my approach. I began focusing my discussions with her on facts and analysis, rather than concepts or strategy. As a result of coming to comprehend *her* way of thinking, my ability to communicate positively with her improved dramatically.

Do you understand how people react to disappointment? Leaders sometimes have to disclose upsetting or disappointing news. You have to understand and be adept at recognizing the emotions people typically go through in reacting to bad news. At first, people often deny the unfortunate reality. Then they will feel angry, and possibly betrayed. Next they may be depressed by it, and then, finally, they will begin to seek solutions to accommodate the new reality.

Your communication style should reflect that you understand these very human responses to disappointment.

ORGANIZE YOUR CONTENT EFFECTIVELY

Once you understand your audience, you are ready to build your communication plan. Use the following approach to organizing the content of your presentation:

- Make a person-to-person connection with your audience.
- Build a broad context to serve as the background for your idea and to frame its importance.
- Describe your idea or product, the opportunities it will create, and the problems it will solve based upon your understanding of your audience.

Make a Person-to-Person Connection with Your Audience

In large group presentations, demonstrating from the outset that you *understand* who the audience is can help build a personal connection with them. This approach is important because it will help the audience to focus on *the rest of your message.* I often found that in one-on-one conversations, if I began by acknowledging the skills or strengths of the individual, the conversation was likely to be more relaxed and productive. Try discussing experiences you've both shared in the past or common problems.

Leadership Insight

People make decisions based on the merits of a proposal and their need to be valued as individuals.

Early in my career, I learned the importance of making a personal connection with my audience in a one-on-one conversation with a senior executive at Coca-Cola. I was trying to convince him to focus more energy on improving the quality of the financial controls inside one international business division. Initially, I centered my conversation on the problem—the breakdowns in controls and the lack of quality financial information coming from his operation. The executive got angry, and I realized I had offended him. The rest of our conversation was unproductive.

I decided to pull back. About a week later, after speaking to this executive's coworkers, I decided to take another approach. This time, I began our discussion by pointing out how he had succeeded with his organization because he was an effective decision maker. I emphasized that I recognized that his influence had dramatically strengthened the operations for which he was responsible. After I recognized his importance to the company and his value as an individual, he relaxed.

Then I pointed out that perhaps we could improve the amount of information that he had available to him about his organization's operational performance. He seemed interested. Therefore, I suggested that having more information—the kind that required stronger information and control systems—would help him make even better and faster decisions. By then he was paying close attention, even nodding in agreement. He understood that improving these systems would be "win-win" for the company and for him.

Key Point

As they listen, people want to be valued for their capabilities, skills, and good personal qualities.

By working to connect with him—and by understanding and acknowledging his skills and strengths as a leader—I was able to offer a scenario that appealed to him and that he would support.

Build a Broad Context

Build a broad context to serve as the background for your idea and to frame its importance to your audience. For example, if you are trying to communicate the importance of a cost-cutting program, you might first discuss how the challenging economic environment might impact the financial performance of your audience's organization. Then you are positioned to propose your program to help address those challenges. Alternatively, if you are selling a new product, you might first discuss the overall changing needs of consumers and how they might impact your audience. Then, describe how your product satisfies those needs. These approaches allow your audience to understand the larger background for your plan, product, or idea.

Describe Your Idea or Product

Describe your idea or product, the opportunities it will create, and the problems it will solve based upon your understanding of your audience. One effective method for discussing your idea or proposal is a communications model developed by Speakeasy Communications Consulting LLC, which I mentioned earlier:

- **Summarize, in one sentence, your idea and the benefits it would bring to your audience.**

  In our first investor presentation at Revlon in 2002, I believe we did a good job of summarizing our idea: Revlon was a company with tremendous "unlocked" value, and that by capitalizing on our strong brands, strengthening our marketing strategy, and by improving in-store execution of our merchandising and marketing programs, shareowner value could be increased over time. The idea of **focusing on basic marketing strategy and execution,** both important elements of our business that were within our control, to **unlock value and potentially build long-term stock price appreciation** was simple. It encouraged investors to listen for how we would do it.

- **Answer, in your remarks that follow the opening summary of your idea, the questions you believe will be on the listeners' minds once they have heard your opening statement.**

  If you are selling the benefits of a new software program, the questions you might expect to be on your audience's mind following the opening summary of your idea would include:

  - What exactly will the program *do* for my specific business?
  - What makes it better than other software?
  - What hardware will the program work on?
  - What are the purchase and conversion costs?
  - What are the ongoing expenses?

  Call out, address, and answer these questions in the body of your presentation. If you properly anticipate and address the questions that would be on the minds of your listeners, you are likely to be an effective influencer. This approach worked well at the Revlon investor presentation. We anticipated the following questions:

  - What are the basic execution issues that have held Revlon back?
  - Once those execution issues have been solved, do you have the assets (e.g., brands) to build upon and generate future growth?
  - With an understanding of the issues and the assets you have to build upon, do you have the management team that can execute the plan to capitalize on these assets?
  - What are the risks that this plan cannot be executed successfully?
  - What value can be created if indeed the plan is executed successfully?

  By anticipating and answering these questions, we put ourselves in the best position to convince our audience that our core idea—in this case that tremendous unlocked value could emerge from improved marketing strategies and execution—was believable.

- **Once you have answered, in the body of your presentation, the questions you anticipated from your audience then move to your closing remarks.**
  Your closing statements should be designed to reconnect your idea and the audience to the broader context that you provided as a background for your idea. Remind the listeners of the challenges you discussed and how your idea represents the ideal solution to those challenges. Finally, take care to *reconnect on a personal level* with your audience. After all, people buy ideas and things from people they perceive as trustworthy and sincere.

Key Questions to Consider

Are you "overprepared" for your communication? The best presenters show flexibility and have the ability to react in the moment. This requires focusing on the audience and observing how they are responding to your communication. The ability to think on your feet comes in part from *overpreparation on the basics* of your presentation beforehand. Often early in my career, my colleagues kidded me about always seeming to overrehearse for presentations. I did that because I was taught that by being well versed in the basic content materials, you can employ your energy to *focus on your audience,* rather than worry about the specifics of your remarks. This helps you to be really responsive to your audience and adjust your prepared presentation based on what you are seeing or hearing. Overpreparing—allowing you the time, energy, and ability to react to the moment at hand as needed—can be an enormous help to the overall success of your presentation.

Are you using analogies to reinforce your point? People internalize information in different ways. Try using analogies from different environments, such as sports, history, and other parts of your audience's everyday life or experiences. This opens another potential pathway for effective communication. Sometimes, people are influenced by an analogy that is not particularly related to the situation at hand, because they can think about what is being said logically, and not be weighed down by the detailed specifics of your proposal immediately.

A word of caution: If you are presenting in a different country, culture, or language, consider beforehand that comments and analogies considered ordinary in your environment might not work, or translate, as well with a different audience.

Are you allowing enough time for people to process what you have told them? People need time to embrace new ideas. Give people a chance to digest what you are communicating. In a small group or one-on-one dialogue, check people on their understanding by asking them questions that will get them to summarize what they have heard. This will also help cement their understanding of what you said.

During intense negotiations, once you have made a significant amount of progress and have "moved the ball" in a positive direction, suggest taking a break. This gives people time to solidify in their minds what has been agreed upon and refresh themselves before you move on.

Are you continually aware of the reaction of your audience? You should look for reactions from your audience—facial expressions, body language—that signal confusion or misunderstanding. If you see this, move to clarify or reinforce an important point. If you see reactions like disinterest, sleepiness, or people checking their BlackBerries, it may signal that it's time to take a break, sum up, or regroup.

If an audience member seems to react negatively to one of your key points, you may look for an opportunity to readdress that point later in your remarks, or after the presentation in a question-and-answer period.

Are you staying the course with your communication? It is very important to have conviction and be appropriately persistent about your ideas in order to effectively communicate.

At Revlon, our consistent message was that by focusing on our consumers, our customers, and our own organization, and by working to strengthen our business with these three constituencies, we could create tremendous success for our company. We constantly addressed exactly what we were doing to drive the business in these important areas. For example, our quarterly earnings announcements and our employee updates were always organized in this fashion.

We measured and communicated positive results against these three strategic building blocks; negative results were discussed in much the same way. Our communication was frequent and sometimes seemed repetitive. But we were always consistent in saying that focusing on these three areas would bring success. By doing so, we encouraged employees to focus their actions in these three areas.

Are you thoroughly addressing the questions of the most analytical (and sometimes seemingly cynical) members of your audience? In most audiences, there will be at least one cynic, but these people often ask discerning questions that are important to others who may have questions lurking in their minds that they were afraid to ask publicly.

I have seen many senior leaders be dismissive of a tough, analytical questioner and turn off an entire audience. Treat these questions and the questioners with the respect they deserve. These situations can create opportunity to influence an audience. Your answers and the tone you use in responding to their questions may be the key to how the majority in the room evaluates you and whether they open their minds to your ideas. There is a certain amount of "group identification" psychology present in every audience that must be recognized and respected.

Key Point

Focus on the broadcast towers and on the most analytical members of your audience. They often are the ones that most influence others in the audience.

Are you using letters, informal "drop-ins," and other forms of communication to get your message out? Remember, it is essential that you spend time talking with people and reinforcing your key messages. If you recall from the experience I described earlier when as a fairly new employee of Coca-Cola I received a letter from the chairman complimenting me on a presentation, you can take advantage of opportunities to acknowledge your employees' good work through written correspondence. You can also use informal lunches and other casual meetings to elicit opinions, give attention to their concerns and challenges, and provide feedback.

While I was at Revlon, we decided to recruit for several key marketing and sales positions. However, the company was having trouble attracting the kind of talent we were seeking. So one day I stopped by to see the head of our recruiting department. After this "drop-in," I realized that I had not been paying enough attention to this critical function. I learned that we were significantly understaffed with recruiters to meet the challenge of hiring a significant number of marketing and salespeople. At the same time, the recruiters that we had did not have adequate materials describing the company's progress to demonstrate to potential recruits that Revlon would be an excellent place to further their careers.

After this discussion, we added significant resources—and more leadership oversight—to our recruiting function, including materials describing our progress and opportunities for advancement at Revlon. This adjustment allowed us to attract additional employees of the caliber we desired. This is just one example of the importance of drop-ins, and **taking the time to listen to the challenges of your people.**

Are you using visual aids? Using an easel or whiteboard in one-on-one and small group discussions can enhance the focus on meeting content and reduce potential feelings of confrontation.

Are you prioritizing your audiences? Focus significant time on your highest performers and those that make a real difference to the long-term health of your organization. For example, perhaps you should reallocate more of your time to visiting sales-generating operating units and your key customers.

Are you looking at everyone? Simply making eye contact is one of the most powerful tools of communication. Look people in the eye as you pass in the hall; acknowledge them. Eye contact or a handshake can establish a personal connection. One former senior leader at Coca-Cola had an amazing impact on morale just in the way that he walked the halls and recognized people, if only for a moment each.

BUILD A CONNECTION BETWEEN YOU AND YOUR AUDIENCE

The people you are trying to influence do not want to be held to a standard of perfection; that is impossible. Lead with humility. For you and your audience to relate and connect, they need to know that you do not expect them to be perfect. The best way to do that is to let them know that you are aware of your own limitations. That sense of humility and vulnerability develops a sense of openness with your audience that leads to successful communication.

Leadership Insight

People will be more readily influenced by someone who doesn't pretend to be perfect, who is humble, and doesn't expect perfection from them!

One of the best examples of demonstrating humility (and extremely effective influencing) that I ever saw was when Coca-Cola decided to reverse course and reintroduce "the old Coca-Cola formula" in 1986, in the form of Coca-Cola Classic.

Many American consumers were upset with the company for withdrawing the original formula for Coca-Cola, which they had come to know and love for many years, and replacing it with the "new" Coke. Therefore, when the company decided to bring back the old Coca-Cola, they knew it was important to win back the hearts and minds of the American consumer—particularly those loyal to Coca-Cola products over the years. For this to happen, The Coca-Cola Company had to demonstrate a sense of humility and acknowledge that perhaps it had made an error in judgment when it pulled the old Coca-Cola product from the shelves.

To its credit, The Coca-Cola Company essentially said just that; if they had to do it over again, they would have left the old Coca-Cola on the shelf even while bringing a new Coke product to the marketplace. The admission that we had underestimated the strong feelings Americans had for the original Coca-Cola demonstrated a sense of humility to consumers that almost instantly won over consumers' hearts and minds—and thirsts—when the old Coca-Cola found its way back onto the supermarket shelves.

Key Questions to Consider

Are you using humor and passion, and revealing your personality in your communication? Humor can be an excellent way of breaking tension and helping to get across a complicated idea, as can a sense of passion or commitment. Show people that you really care about an idea, and they will be more likely to think it's important. At Revlon, we had an annual North American sales conference where the marketing department showed new marketing plans. Rather than make their presentations in the traditional format, one year they created a mock news broadcast announcing the marketing news for the upcoming year. The presenters showed sides of their personalities that were not only very funny, but also demonstrated their enthusiasm for their ideas. These presentations were very effective in energizing the salesforce.

Are you showing up for key events and important milestones? People want events that are important to *them* to be important to *you*. For example, you should understand whether it would be meaningful to your customers for you to attend conferences, trade shows, and conventions that they host. Though it's expensive, sometimes traveling a long distance to attend a customer's key event can send a strong message to the customer about how much you value them.

Are you "overdisclosing"? Take some risk in terms of how much you disclose about your thoughts, feelings, and the reasons behind your thinking. People will better connect to your ideas and to you as a leader. My own experience suggests that demonstrating trust invites the same from your listener.

Are you publicly giving people credit for their accomplishments? This seems obvious but you can sometimes "value" the whole group when people hear others receiving credit for good work. For example, as I mentioned earlier, Revlon held routine meetings with our employees to update our people on the company's progress. Then we switched to letting employees be the main speakers at these meetings. It was a very positive experience for the employees to learn that management appreciated them and their efforts to develop new ideas and solutions to move the business forward. Whenever we had a chance to recognize by name an individual who had created success, we looked for ways to do it during these employee conferences. It created tremendous goodwill. It also encourages other people to find ways to move the business forward even faster.

Are you making sure not to publicly embarrass people when finding a mistake or problem? Working to understand the *underlying systemic reason* for a problem so that changes can be made to how work gets done is very important. In this situation, it can be worthwhile to call out significant lessons from that breakdown publicly in order to avoid repeating it. Yet, if the mistake occurred **due to a skill gap**

or deficiency in a particular person, my experience is that the first discussion should be with that person privately. One-on-one communication will likely be more successful in motivating the individual to improve needed skills. Publicly embarrassing someone often makes that person (and others around) withdraw, and prevents them from taking more effective action in the future. When I'd made the mistake of publicly embarrassing someone, I often found that it took significant time for me to repair the damage I had done.

CLOSING STATEMENT

The approaches to influencing people that I discussed suggest that people evaluate ideas and proposals based on two concepts: 1) the merits of the proposal or idea itself, and 2) their basic need to be valued as individuals. To summarize:

- Take the time in advance to gain an understanding of your audience.
  - Identify their beliefs, goals, motivations, strategies, and challenges.
  - Determine how they might personally "win" through your proposal.
  - Understand any assumptions they may already have about the ideas you are about to discuss.
- Have a clear picture of what you are trying **to persuade your audience to think or do,** and be thoughtful about how you organize your content in order to achieve that goal.
- Build a connection between you and your audience.

Conclusion

Building the right environment to achieve outstanding results requires creating and communicating a clear picture of your organization's destination and plan, developing a capable team of skilled people, and executing successfully. Leading effectively and building capabilities is not complicated, but it is *very hard work*. It requires attention to the details of your plan. It calls for attracting, motivating, and retaining capable people, and helping that team develop by giving them assignments and coaching that will build their skills. Of course, it also requires that you develop and capitalize on your own skills as a leader and leverage the inherent strengths you bring as a result of your background, experiences, and personality.

Creating results that are better than you expected is tremendously satisfying, as is developing a legacy of capable, motivated people. I hope these frameworks help you, as they have helped me, find that satisfaction.

Valuing a Business Using the Discounted Cash Flow Approach

The two Appendixes presented here are derived from basic finance theory learned in university studies. You can find similar material in textbooks like *Essentials of Managerial Finance*, by J. Fred Weston and Eugene F. Brigham (Dryden Press, 1993). In these areas, you should always seek help from a financial professional. Following are the key steps of one accepted way of valuing a business, the *discounted cash flow approach*:

1. **Project the future annual cash inflows expected to be generated by the business before interest or principal payments on borrowed funds and excluding any noncash "bookkeeping" charges, including depreciation or amortization and before dividends to shareowners**—In other words, *cash inflows* equal after-tax profits *before* interest, depreciation, amortization, or any other noncash charges. As cash inflow grows, so does value.

2. **Project the business's future annual cash outflows**—Cash outflows equal the total of expected capital spending required for fixed assets, such as plant and equipment, plus any

anticipated necessary increases in working capital (accounts receivable, inventories, etc.).

3. **Subtract the annual cash outflows projected for each future year from the annual cash inflows**—What is left over is *"free cash flow,"* the funds available each year for interest and principal repayments, dividends, and for the company, if it chooses, to buy back its own stock. **As *free cash flow* grows, so does the value of the business.**

   Typically, when free cash flows are projected, they are forecasted for the current year, and then for the following nine years, or ten years in total. There is no "magic" to forecasting for this number of years. If your business is likely to see dramatic shifts for periods that go beyond ten years, then a longer forecasting model might be appropriate.

4. **Discount *each year's* projected *free cash flow* using the rate of the company's overall cost of capital to bring its *future value* back to today's *present value***—As noted in step 3, the free cash flow is *the difference between each future year's projected cash inflow and cash outflow.* When the *present value* of a future free cash flow is calculated, it will be smaller than the projected *future* free cash flow amount. That is because if you already had the smaller, discounted amount today, you could immediately begin to invest it to earn a return. You would expect over time that the value of that investment would increase to its *future value* amount. Therefore, in exchange for your right to receive a *future year's* projected free cash flow at that point in the future, you would accept now the calculated discounted *present value* amount as being of equivalent value today.

   The annual *rate* by which a future year's free cash flow is discounted to determine today's present value is equal to the company's overall *cost of capital.* This cost of capital, or "discount rate," for a typical large, U.S.-based corporation, ranges between 6 percent and 10 percent. (The concept and method of calculation of the *cost of capital* appropriate for your business is discussed in more detail in Appendix B.) Use your company's cost of capital as the discount rate to discount the free cash flows of each of Years One through Ten (in this example) back to today's present value.

The current (or Year One) cash flow is discounted by multiplying the projected free cash flow in Year One by 1 minus the *discount rate*. For example, if the discount rate is 10 percent, or 0.10, then multiply Year One's free cash flow by 0.90 (1.0 – 0.10) to get the present value of Year One's free cash flow. To get the present value of Year Two's free cash flow, multiply that amount by one minus the discount rate (0.90) *twice,* because that free cash flow must be discounted backward from Year *Two,* to get the *present value* of that year's free cash flow. Therefore, Year Two's projected free cash flow—let's say it's $100— is multiplied by 0.90, and then again by 0.90, to get the *present value* of Year Two's projected free cash flow, which would be $81 {[($100 × 0.90) × 0.90] = $81}. Year Three's protected free cash flow would be discounted three times, and this pattern would continue until the Year Ten free cash flow, which would be discounted *ten separate times.*

5. **Add together these ten discounted annual free cash flows, or present values**—The total equals the *present value of the free cash flows* for the business for the forecast period.

6. **Now calculate the "terminal value" and the *present value* of the terminal value for the business**—The terminal value for the business is the projected remaining value of the business at the *end* of the period for which you have forecasted free cash flows. There are a number of ways to project the so-called "terminal value" of a business, and as in other parts of this analysis, typically would require the help of a financial expert. Generally, however, the terminal value of a business can be projected in two ways. The first is to take the free cash flow in the last forecast year and divide that free cash flow by the cost of capital, or discount rate. This values the free cash flow of the company at the end of the

forecasting period as if it were an annuity that would continue out into perpetuity (an annuity which is to be paid in perpetuity, consisting of a known future annual cash flow amount, is valued by taking the annual payment amount and dividing it by the discount rate). The resulting amount is the projected terminal value of the business at the *end* of the forecasting period.

Another way to project the terminal value of a business is to "benchmark" the business's value against the *trading values* of other like businesses. For example, if the business you're in typically trades on a stock exchange for two times net revenues, you could use that to determine the projected terminal value for your business. To do that, multiply your forecast of net revenues for Year Ten by two in order to calculate a projected terminal value.

By choosing one of the above methods, you can project a *terminal value* for your business, which is the second component of coming up with a value for your business. However, keep in mind that, once you have projected the terminal value of the business at the end of the forecast period, say ten years, **that terminal value itself needs to be discounted back to today's value, just as you did with each of the ten years of free cash flows, using your discount rate.** In this case, the projected terminal value at the end of Year Ten would be discounted ten separate times, in order to determine the *present value of the terminal value.*

Now you have obtained the two components required to arrive at the overall total value, or *"enterprise value"* of a business.

7. **Calculate the total value, or *enterprise value*, of your business**—To do this add the *present value of the free cash flows* for the business, as calculated in step number 5—together with the *present value of the terminal value,* obtained by whichever method you chose in step number 6. **The resulting total is the *enterprise value* of the business.**

Note: You may need to adjust the enterprise value upward if the business owns any assets—such as real estate, excess cash, or financial investments not required to operate the business—whose values are not adequately reflected in the business's projections for future cash inflows. Similarly, you may need to adjust the enterprise value downwards if the business has any potential liabilities, or other financial exposures, not adequately reflected in the projection of future annual cash outflows.

8. **Determine the shareowners' interest in the business**—Finally, in order to determine the value of the *shareowners'* interest in the business, subtract from the *enterprise value* of the business *any debt owed.* What remains is the *present value of the equity owned by the shareowners.*

Determining the Cost of Capital

You can create *significant value* for your company by having a capital structure that is appropriate for your business and **reduces the cost of your company's cost of capital.**

Your company's overall cost of capital is equal to the *average annual rate of return that those who provide funds to your company expect to earn over time.* There are two basic sources of funds for your business: 1) borrowed funds, or debt, and 2) equity capital provided by shareowners. Therefore, the most important decision when creating a capital structure for your business is the mix between debt and shareowner equity.

There are two principal factors that determine the appropriate balance of debt and equity capital for your business:

1. The cost of each form of capital

2. Whether or not your company's earnings stream is predictable and stable enough to be able to meet the fixed interest and principal payments related to debt

Your company's after-tax cost of debt equals the interest rate your lenders charge, minus the reduction in the *actual cost* to your business that occurs because interest payments are generally tax deductible. For calculating the after-tax cost of debt, generally the cost of long-term debt is used because that is the type of debt that companies predominantly use in their capital structures. For example, if your company's long-term borrowing rate is 9 percent and your overall tax rate is 40 percent, your *after-tax cost of borrowed funds* is 5.4 percent, or [9 percent × (1 – 0.40)].

Shareowners expect an even higher average annual return on their investment over time due to the greater risk of investing in common stocks (equities). They expect to realize their higher return through *increases in the market value* of their investment, and perhaps through *dividends* paid to them by the company in which they've invested, both of which they understand can be subject to a significant degree of volatility and risk. Due to this risk, shareowners expect to earn a rate of return significantly higher than a "risk-free" investment, such as a long-term government bond. In other words, they demand a rate of return "premium" to compensate for the greater risk. Historically, the required equity risk premium a shareowner seeks to earn above the annual return on a risk-free investment, such as a government bond, is 4 to 5 percent for an equity security of a company that has risk characteristics equal to the stock market as a whole.

Therefore, when long-term government bonds offer an anticipated return of 8 percent, the total average annual return that would be expected by an equity investor equals approximately 13 percent, after including a 5 percent risk premium.

CALCULATE YOUR COMPANY'S OVERALL COST OF CAPITAL

Your company's overall cost of capital is the average of the cost of debt and the cost of equity capital, weighted by the proportion that each represents in your capital structure. For example, in a capital structure that is made up of 50 percent debt at an after cost of 5.4 percent (as calculated earlier), and 50 percent equity at a cost of

13 percent, the overall cost of capital is 9.2 percent, which equals the weighted average of the cost of debt and equity [(50 percent × 5.4 percent) + (50 percent × 13 percent)].

Because debt costs less than equity capital, using an appropriate amount of debt will reduce your company's overall cost of capital and therefore increase the value of your company. The percentage of your capital structure that can be made up of debt depends on the stability of your company's earnings stream and its ability to meet interest and principal obligations.

Knowing your overall cost of capital is important because this is the minimum required rate of return, or hurdle rate, you should seek on investments of capital (e.g., investments in fixed assets) in your business. If capital investments in your business earn this minimum rate of return, they will **generate enough funds back to enable it to satisfy its obligations to both lenders and shareowners.**

In most environments, your company would aggressively seek to maximize investments that offer returns above your cost of capital and are in line with your business strategy. This would be expected to enhance the value of your business. In contrast, the value of your business will likely decline if your organization continuously invests in projects earning less than your overall cost of capital. By doing so, you will not meet the expectations of your shareowners and perhaps not be able to meet the interest and principal obligations to your lenders. It is also important to point out that you should demand an even higher rate of return than your company's overall cost of capital for projects or investments that have above-average risk associated with them. Your financial advisors can help with this assessment.

It is important to communicate to your financial organization the minimum *required rate of return* (hurdle rate) on your company's investment of capital. Your organization should understand the importance of **not committing resources to low-return projects**—in other words, projects with projected rates of return below your company's overall cost of capital—unless there is some other compelling reason to do so.

Executive Abstract—
Quick Reference Guide

FRAMEWORK 1:
LEADERSHIP AND MANAGEMENT

Set a compelling destination for your organization.

- Are you involving others in the development of your destination statement?

Develop a clear and focused strategy.

- Are you making the tough choices about which options to pursue?

Set measurable objectives for getting there.

- Are you setting objectives that will appropriately "push" your organization?

Develop a thorough plan to execute your strategy.

- **Assets**—What do you have to work with to achieve your strategy?
- **Action steps**—Who must take what specific steps and by when?

- **Barriers**—What can stand in your way?
- **Resources and solutions**—How can you overcome the barriers?
- **Expectations and returns**—What do you expect to gain financially or in marketplace results?

Communicate your strategy for reaching your destination.

- Are you doing enough listening?
- Are you using visible signals to demonstrate your direction?
- Are you persistent in telling the story?
- Are you managing perceptions, or being victimized by them?
- Are you using comparisons that help people understand your strategy and what you expect it to deliver?
- Are members of your leadership team following your example in embracing and communicating your organization's destination and strategy?

Execute details and review your progress.

- Are your employees sweating the details?
- Are you automatically assuming good execution?
- Are you relentless?
- Are you looking for the cracks?
- Are you relying exclusively on company manuals and rulebooks to guide your people?
- Do you act fast?

Build and utilize effective control and information reporting systems.

- Do your control and information reporting systems support your key strategies and plans?

Actively develop the organization and the people who can help reach the destination.

- Are you staying in close touch with your people?

Key Points

- A modest view of your future brings modest results and rewards. Think big and give people the opportunity to win big.
- Develop a clear strategy that will galvanize people and require them to focus on the right actions for success.
- Require staff functions to develop clear plans to achieve your organization's overall objectives and strategies.
- Focus extra attention on areas of your organization where the details are not being closely reviewed and managed.
- Develop clear and simple key principles or values to guide the day-to-day behaviors that will create success for your organization.

Leadership Insights

- People want to work toward or invest in ideas that are exciting and that they can visualize. Paint a compelling picture of *what that success will look and feel like* to your people.
- If leaders aren't bold in setting a destination, no one else will be!
- Quantifying a goal forces clarity in discussions about what is possible and what is required to achieve it.
- Understanding where people stand on an issue allows you to develop a plan to influence where they end up.
- Early in a change process, it is critical to take actions that demonstrate your direction clearly. People are looking for visible signals of change and progress.
- Successful execution of important plans and projects requires a leader's attention to detail. Be attentive and others will follow your lead—and your business will benefit.

FRAMEWORK 2:
CREATING A HIGH-CAPABILITY ORGANIZATION

Communicate the opportunity for your business and its people.

- Are you involving all of your people in the process of defining the strategy to reach the destination of your organization?

Be visible to the people in your organization.

Present a clear picture of the core skills required for success in your organization.

1. The ability to learn from, observe, and question the environment around you
2. The ability to see opportunities
3. The ability to develop a detailed plan and organize the necessary resources for action
4. The ability to execute a plan and focus on the details
5. The ability to effectively communicate and work as part of a team
6. The ability to recognize and develop the skills of others

- Do your employees clearly understand what skills and performance will determine their success within your organization?

Recruit and assign jobs based on the necessary skills to succeed.

- Are your hiring managers (with support from your human resources team) able to clearly define and communicate the core skills necessary for success in your organization to those who will be recruiting and interviewing candidates to fill those needs?
- Are you relying on soft information, or unclear communication, when interviewing a potential employee?

Invest in and capitalize on diversity.

- Are you investing strongly in diversity?

Key Points

- Do whatever it takes to help every single person understand your organization's direction and destination.
- Create easy channels for feedback to ensure that your people understand where the organization is going and that they can influence its direction. Don't allow lack of communication by you and your leadership team to be an excuse for lack of performance or results!
- There is no substitute for people who are willing and able to complete effectively both detailed grunt work and high-level work, in a timely way, and in different environments.
- Grow the capabilities of your organization by ensuring that you have managers who can attract and develop strong people.
- Participate in the interview process for critical roles.
- Require that interviewees give you very specific examples of when, where, and how they have demonstrated the behaviors and actions required for success in the potential new assignment.

Leadership Insights

- People and organizations develop faster with encouragement, when they have a sense of direction, and when they are heard.
- In leadership, visibility counts! It demonstrates that you take seriously the importance of working together to reach your organization's destination.
- People focus on those skills and behaviors that leaders say count.
- Ultimately, your objective should be to make your people even more effective than you, their leader, are.

- Recruiting and staffing need not be a hit-or-miss process. There is a logical approach to putting the right people into the right roles.
- Success is often the result of different ideas arising from different perspectives. Seek out—and capitalize on—a diverse workforce.

FRAMEWORK 3:
DEVELOPING PEOPLE

Comprehend the difference between core skills and exposure.

Create opportunities for both project and process experience.

- Does your organization have a way for its cross-functional leadership to discuss open job positions and to surface potential candidates from across the organization to fill them?

Use an effective model for feedback and appraisals.

1. Value the individual and his or her strengths and contributions.
2. Ask the person to assess his or her own performance and to discuss where he or she is encountering the greatest challenges in the job.
3. Provide clear and pointed feedback relative to the critical skill or area of performance where you want to see improvement.
4. Agree on the areas of focus and skill development for the future.
5. Agree on the benefits of improving and the consequences of not improving certain skills.
6. Commit your support for and reiterate the value of the individual.

- Are you being consistent in the feedback that you provide an individual about your expectations?
- Are you dealing with development issues immediately?

Utilize control systems as development tools.

1. Create opportunities for joint learning.
2. Allow the discovery of new facts and insights.
3. Assist in the continued development of people.

Be situational in your management style.

- Are you focusing enough of your management time on the strong performers in your organization?

Manage compensation strategically.

Use mistakes strategically.

Key Points

- An important oversight technique for major projects is to schedule frequent project updates, and be sure that when someone says something is done, it is totally complete.
- People's ability to generate results usually grows in a gradual fashion, not in big jumps. Reward results and growth in skills.

Leadership Insights

- Working against intense deadlines creates pressure that, if managed effectively, can contribute to personal growth.
- Core skills translate across most departments and organizations.
- Development occurs through frequent problem-solving and coaching conversations with experienced and skilled leaders in an organization.
- Capitalize on every opportunity to develop people—*it's worth it.*

FRAMEWORK 4:
BRAND POSITIONING WITH CONSUMERS

Define what your product or service uniquely delivers to your target consumers.

- Have you defined what your brand delivers—physically and emotionally?
- Are you being persistent in telling your consumers what benefits your product or service offers them?

Define and focus your marketing on your target consumers.

- Have you clearly defined your target market?
- Are you working to deliver your brand's promise to your loyal consumers?

Create a name and visual appearance for your brand that reinforces its positioning.

Build your brand at the point of purchase.

- If you are selling packaged consumer products, are you working with your retail partners to strengthen how your brand is presented to the consumer at the point of purchase?

Build marketing relationships for your brand that resonate with your target consumers.

Prioritize and sequence the actions to reinforce your brand positioning.

Avoid positioning leakage in marketing and advertising.

- Who in your organization "owns" your brand and is responsible for briefing your advertising and marketing agencies?

Build new layers into your brand.

- Are you finding new ways to reinforce your bond with your consumers?
- Are you allowing your expenditures to work twice?

Be aware of those chipping into the positioning of your brand.

- Are you aware of your competitors and their brands' strengths?

Be disciplined with your marketing resources.

Key Points

- Strong marketing power is the result of taking the time to develop a clear and concise positioning for your brand.
- Throughout every one of your marketing programs, take care to reinforce exactly what your brand *delivers to your consumers.*
- Marketing resources usually are limited. Be clear about who your target consumers are and focus your limited resources on them.
- Your trademark visuals, graphics, and packaging choices should be carefully selected and designed to reinforce the overall positioning of your brand.
- Focus on creating consumer benefits that relate to *how* a product is purchased; this can be a very effective and efficient form of marketing.
- Every brand marketing relationship either builds on or detracts from your brand. Choose only relationships that are consistent with the positioning of your brand.
- Prioritize your potential marketing programs and then focus on quality execution of the program(s) you've selected. This will maximize impact on the marketplace and the growth of your brands.

Leadership Insights

- While success in business depends on *action,* at the heart of exceptional marketing is *clear thinking,* particularly when you focus on how to position a brand.
- Focusing on your consumers' lifestyles, their daily routines, and their emotional needs will help you shape *what* your product can deliver to them.
- Your competitors are probably thinking clearly about *your* consumers and their needs. You should do it *first* and *constantly!*
- Often people in organizations will choose brand relationships based on their own personal interests. Make sure the relationships you choose are focused *solely on what builds and reinforces your brand.*
- Prioritizing where to commit limited resources, capability, and time—to achieve maximum results—is one of your most important roles as a leader.
- There is enormous value in long-living, enduring brands. Sometimes your organization will need to be nudged to focus on sustaining and building an established brand when there might be more excitement, but less *value,* in marketing a new brand.

FRAMEWORK 5:
CUSTOMER RELATIONSHIP MANAGEMENT

Understand your customer.

Understand what your customer really wants to buy and why.

Prioritize your customer base.

- Do you have a good understanding of the economics involved in serving a potential or current customer?

Identify the people who influence decisions about your product or service.

1. The Economic Buyer
2. The User Buyer
3. The Technical Buyer
4. The Coach

Listen for opportunities.

- If your customers are retailers, are you visiting their locations and outlets?

Develop a selling strategy.

- Are you focusing on any potential barriers that may exist to positioning and selling your product to the customer successfully?

Present your proposal to the customer.

- Are you considering the proper timing for your proposal?
- Does your presentation focus on the customer's opportunities and problems, and not yours?
- Have you presold your proposal?
- Are you demonstrating passion for your product or service?
- Are there points that are so important to your organization that you must fall on your sword rather than relinquish ground?
- Are you demonstrating that you understand your customers are people too?
- As you present your strategy for bringing solutions to the customer, are you making it their strategy?

Develop plans and execute agreements.

- Are you completing contracts with your customers quickly?

Schedule stewardship and review meetings.

- Are you personally keeping in touch with your organization's key customers?
- Can you create exclusive currencies for your customers in order to increase mutual value?
- Are you always looking for additional ways to build new layers of strength into your customer relationships?

Key Points

- Constantly take steps to strengthen your relationships with your customers. If not, your customers will commit more of their energy and business to those suppliers who do.
- Develop a solid selling strategy which supports your destination and plan for your customer.
- As a leader, stay up to date on your organization's relationships with key customers; feedback can represent threats—or opportunities—for you and your business.
- Listen closely to learn about the *little things* you can do as an added service for your customer. They may be *big* for them!

Leadership Insights

- Asking questions and listening patiently and carefully—in order to understand your customer's business, where they want to take it, and how well you are serving it—is the foundation for great customer service.
- Your customer typically has two ways to win—professionally and personally. Listening for both will create opportunities to serve your customer more effectively.
- As a leader, part of your responsibility is to ensure that your organization is prioritizing where and how its resources are invested with customers.
- Customers *want to be sold to,* and like everyone else, they want to be valued. Making a personal connection to your customers is critical to understanding their needs.

■ Execution is critical! Recognize that many people will have more energy and enthusiasm for making the sale than for finalizing the details of the agreement—or for overseeing its operational execution—with the customer.

FRAMEWORK 6:
FINANCIAL STRATEGY AND MANAGEMENT

Identify the primary goal of your organization.

Know how to determine the value of a business.

Develop a model that links the drivers of your business to how value is created for shareowners.

■ Does your organization have a narrow-minded focus on earnings per share as the only key indicator of performance?

Put in place financial policies that create value and are appropriate for your business.

■ Are your company's financial policies and strategies standing in the way of creating value?

Encourage financial people to have an attitude of service, versus one of control.

Encourage financial people to focus on the economics of the business and value creation.

Communicate effectively with investors.

Build effective control and information reporting systems.

Recognize the importance of the many functional disciplines in your organization.

Create compensation systems that link to shareowner value.

Key Points

- The goal of creating value for those who own your business through growth in free cash flow is fundamental to strong financial strategy and management.
- Long-term cash flow is king!
- Be disciplined about not committing resources to low-return capital projects and investments.
- Setting your dividend payout ratio too high and underinvesting in your business reduces shareowner value. Paying out too little in dividends in order to invest in off-strategy or low-return projects also reduces value.
- The more work investors put into productively studying and understanding your company, the less likely they will be to withdraw their support without solid reasons.
- Explain the control systems of your organization as a *critical tool* for managing your business. You will set the proper tone for the management of your company.

Leadership Insights

- Leaders who understand that financial strategies and controls fuel company success will be best positioned to maximize their organization's long-term value.
- As the leader, you must help make clear to your people the link between their actions and the creation of value for your company.
- People will find lots of reasons for limiting communication with investors. Thoughtful and open communication will help achieve a fair valuation for your stock.

- In order to add maximum value *and* provide controls, the orientation of financial people should be on control through *service,* as opposed to service through *control.*
- The sum total of the elements comprising your control and information systems represents a *management system.*

FRAMEWORK 7:
INFLUENCING PEOPLE

Understand your audience.

- Are you aware of the perceptions of your audience?
- Are you arriving well before your presentations, talking to people who likely will be members of your audience, and asking questions that will help you understand their perceptions, goals, strategies, and challenges?
- Are you staying late after presentations?
- Are you aware of who in your audience are the broadcast towers?
- Do you recognize that people communicate in different ways?
- Do you understand how people react to disappointment?

Organize your content effectively.

- Are you overprepared for your communication?
- Are you using analogies to reinforce your point?
- Are you allowing enough time for people to process what you have told them?
- Are you continually aware of the reaction of your audience?
- Are you staying the course with your communication?
- Are you thoroughly addressing the questions of the most analytical (and sometimes seemingly cynical) members of your audience?
- Are you using letters, informal drop-ins, and other forms of communication to get your message out?

- Are you using visual aids?
- Are you prioritizing your audiences?
- Are you looking at everyone?

Build a connection between you and your audience.

- Are you using humor and passion, and revealing your personality in your communication?
- Are you showing up for key events and important milestones?
- Are you overdisclosing?
- Are you publicly giving people credit for their accomplishments?
- Are you making sure not to publicly embarrass people when finding a mistake or a problem?

Key Points

- Your ability to influence and to be influenced will be either an enabler or a barrier to your success as a leader.
- Understanding your audience, organizationally and personally, is the key to effective communication.
- Seek to understand the motivations of your important audiences, in order to create a platform for effective communication.
- As they listen, people want to be valued for their capabilities, skills, and good personal qualities.
- Focus on the broadcast towers, and on the most analytical members of your audience. They often are the ones that most influence others in the audience.

Leadership Insights

- Immediately creating a picture of what success looks like— for the organization and the individual—positions leaders to influence others to move toward creating that success.

- People make decisions based on the merits of a proposal and their need to be valued as individuals.
- People will more readily be influenced by someone who doesn't pretend to be perfect, who is humble, and doesn't expect perfection from them!

Appendix A: Valuing a Business Using the Discounted Cash Flow Approach.

Appendix B: Determining the Cost of Capital.

Index